AGAINST
THE CURRENT

Phoneme Media
1551 Colorado Blvd., Ste 201
Los Angeles, CA 90041

First Edition, 2016

Published by arrangement with Editorial Era

Translation © Wendy Burk 2016

ISBN: 978-1-939419-78-1

This book is distributed by Publishers Group West

Cover art by Verónica Gerber Bicecci
Cover design and typesetting by Jaya Nicely

Printed in the United States of America

Phoneme Media is a nonprofit media company,
a fiscally sponsored project of Pen Center USA,
dedicated to publishing world literature in translation.

http://phoneme.media

Curious books for curious people.

TEDI LÓPEZ MILLS

AGAINST
THE CURRENT

TRANSLATED FROM THE
SPANISH BY WENDY BURK

A los personajes

To the characters

ACKNOWLEDGEMENTS

Against the Current was originally published in Spanish as *Contracorriente* (Mexico City: Ediciones Era/CONACULTA, 2006) and received the 2008 Premio Nacional de Literatura José Fuentes Mares.

The author and translator gratefully acknowledge the following literary journals, in which many of the translations first appeared, often in different forms or with different titles: *Asymptote, Aufgabe, Cerise Press, The Drunken Boat, The Literary Review,* and *The Volta.*

The translator gratefully acknowledges the support of a 2013 Literature Fellowship in Translation from the National Endowment for the Arts, which made this translation project possible. She also expresses her gratitude to Simmons B. Buntin, Rebecca Seiferle, Lisa Bowden, Kore Press, the University of Arizona Poetry Center, and Eric Magrane for their longtime encouragement of the project. Hearty thanks to Tedi López Mills, David Shook, Jen Lagedrost, Jaya Nicely, and all at Phoneme Media.

TRANSLATOR'S INTRODUCTION

Against the Current is a baroque and speculative work, toned with deep skepticism. Its principal mood is the subjunctive, the mode of futurity, contingency, and wishful thinking. In this, her eighth book of poems, celebrated Mexican author Tedi López Mills uses forceful, intricate fancies to engage a sequence of deeply felt problems, from political to familial and existential to ecological.

"One has to be part of the problem, not part of the solution."[1] López Mills, in so saying, positions herself within a discussion in progress in Mexican literary circles about poetry's relationship to political activism, chiefly activism against systemic violence and corruption. Mistrustful of rallying cries regardless of the merit of the cause, she draws a cynical connection between activist poetry and an ego-driven desire for popularity at public events and literary festivals. López Mills casts activist poetry at best as overly simplistic, and at worst as "demagogical: one includes all the good causes in one's poems so as to get strong approval and applause when one reads out loud."[2]

Although *Against the Current*, originally published in 2006, predates some of this discussion, the statement "One has to be part of the problem" and its literary context are pertinent to the book. Its poems, by being unwieldy, angry, and impossible to summarize, truncated one moment and difficult to contain the next, serve to render the problem glaringly, sometimes burlesquely apparent. In this way they mainly work to problematize problems, rather than to reproduce them.

The problems of which *Against the Current* forms a part include how to be, how to love, how to acknowledge violence,

1 "Poetry As the Site of a Collision: An Interview with Mexican Poet Tedi López Mills." Interview conducted by Wendy Burk. *Cerise Press* 5.13 (2013): n. pag. Web.

2 Ibid.

how to compass identity, and how to exist alongside the non-human. The biggest one, I believe, as introduced by the central character of the brother in relationship to the speaker, and by the central allegory of a wrathful, elusive river, is how to be angry—how to be furious; and yet how to contain this fury, channel it within the confines of a human person who can be, albeit tenuously, recognized as such. Because the poems distrust any form of direct advice, even when it is offered from oneself to oneself, in *Against the Current* to say "How to" is also to imply its opposite: how to not love, for example, or how to not be.

As the title suggests, to read *Against the Current* is to undertake a productive struggle. The book proposes a pessimistic reading of reality, in which cynicism and falsehoods predominate. Within the pessimism, there is possibility. In one sense constrained, and in another unbridled, like water the poems hold so much. Observing the multitude of images float by, we readers can throw in our own concerns and see them become a part of the mix, reflected in the water's mirror.

Mindful of all that this water contains—finely tuned philosophy and allegory, as well as motor oil and plastic bottles, scorn and betrayal, material and emotional detritus—we might choose with care the concerns, desires, and fears that we project onto the poems of *Against the Current*. Rivers flow to the ocean, the source of life; if we throw what we choose into the water, we know where it will be carried.

— Wendy Burk

If I were called in
To construct a religion
I should make use of water.
—Philip Larkin

A

Ríos del agua, ríos solos del agua estrecha, calinosa, arrumbada
entre dos flancos, ríos del agua mala con su fácil lomo reñido
con las trampas, la incierta lámina hacia la retaguardia del día
con sus brotes luminosos bajo el follaje desdibujado por la bruma
que calculo densa cuando la imagino y que atravieso sin dificultad
al pasar por la zona húmeda donde ríos del agua castigan las orillas
con un fango más retráctil, más hambriento, de lodo cerrado
en el jaloneo de las rocas, tirando de las raíces, socavando cualquier
derrotero de la tierra, como si no hubiera distancia mensurable
salvo la que marcan ríos del agua cuando se sueltan de la brecha
con sus aguas invasoras, aguas altas que alteran la áspera topografía
de la breña y lo que uno piensa de los ríos del agua en la cabeza
tantas veces mezclados con su recuerdo y no con los propios
ríos del agua, aún no vistos pero ya oídos: meticulosos,
tímidos, correctos, arponeados por la dulzura del sol
en un perenne mediodía, ríos tan lisos que la mano siempre
se sumerge en la misma agua o en su fantasma y tienta
lo que un tajo de fondo abandona por la superficie,
ríos del agua donde estoy y no he estado nunca, tiempo
de por medio, minuto exacto de un agua distinta, la cohibida
aunque maga a veces cuando traspasa diques, fronteras, murallas
tan antiguas como su meandro, pero dócil agua al cabo, lenta agua
cuando me toca oblicua, me cede una turbulencia mitigada,
río de agua real, río súbito o caudal de plata hacia atrás con su flujo
trabado cribando basura, esquivando lo que mata, lo que tuerce,
lo que se agosta en la sima seca, hebra enjuta con su última gota
en un recodo sin sombras donde los restos de otro río se arremolinan
en la mira y va otra vez con su agua la petición de principio, más sabio
el ojo que la oreja balbuceante con su oro fortuito, más ruidoso

A

Rivers of water, lone rivers of lanky, clouded water, squeezed
by two flanks, rivers of dirty water bucking their easy backs
against traps, dubious metal facing the day's rearguard,
its luminous gush under leaves obscured by a haze
that I imagine as dense and push past smoothly
into the wetlands where rivers of water punish the banks
with their greedy, slurried pulse, mud thickened
in the rocks' drag, uprooting, eroding any
earthly road, as if no distance could ever be measured
except by rivers of water pouring themselves from the breach
with their invading waters, high waters altering the thicket's
rough topography and thoughts about rivers of water in my head
so many times mixed up with memories, not with the rivers
of water themselves, heard but unseen: meticulous,
shy, proper, harpooned by the sweet eternal
noonday sun, rivers so sleek that one's hand always
sinks into the same water or its ghost and gropes
for anything that the depths might release,
rivers of water where I am and have never been, time in between,
clock starting up for a different water, one that hangs back
except when it works its magic breaking levees, crossing borders, scaling
walls as ancient as its meander, but then is gentled, slow water
grazing me, offering up a mitigated turbulence,
river of real water, sudden river or silver surge upstream with its
hobbled flow sifting garbage, skirting what it kills, what it twists,
what it parches in the ditch, trickling its last drop down
to a shadeless bend where the remains of another river eddy
into sight and again with their water beg the question, wiser
the eye than the stammering ear's fortuitous gold, louder

el río circunstancial, los relumbrones divagando hacia una letra, más curva la suerte, casuista la mente: ¿qué es lo que veo, qué es lo que invento?

the circumstantial river, sun's glare digressing towards a letter,

luck's deepest swerve, mind's casuistry: what do I see,

what do I invent?

B

Contémplalo: mi trozo de mundo, mi invertido paraíso de hoja
rala, mi entronque de grava con polvo; mide el día filtrado
por la madera, su tiempo de menos tras la columnata de árboles,
su vestigio de una vista en la reincidencia del campo; huele la peste
en lo que medra, la hierba mala, la hierba de espina, la que se enrosca,
símil más trance, por el rabo en vaivén de una vaca; escucha el timbre
de último día en el mugido, las campanas detrás resonando con ese dolor
semejante, la herida a conciencia que socava el destino desigual
de un cuerpo; y pregunta: ¿qué conoces?
cacharro de mustios reflejos, suena a verdad la mentira: el Ser-ahí
con la sonaja de un pensamiento adentro, leve estribillo: ese soy
lo que soy; vaca, oveja, borrego, el venado de las visiones, el ciervo
de la nieve del poema de una duda: ¿queda vida tras la imagen?
nieve de sol negro escuché alguna vez, promontorio blanco
en la noche; hay cola para presenciar el desenlace; mi paraíso
tendrá los mismos tonos, los mismos matices ideológicos
(mi omisión perpetua ante la causa) que este día de lucro
para la sombra.

B

Consider it: my bit of earth, my inverted paradise bereft
of leaves, where gravel intersects with dust; measure the day filtered
by branches, its time slipping away behind the avenue of trees,
its vestigial panorama in the relapsing field; smell the stench
in what thrives, weeds, burrs, what curls,
simile and trance, around a cow's twitching tail; listen to the last-days
timbre of its lowing, then the bells ringing out with a like
pain, fervent wound eroding the body's fickle
destiny; and ask: what do you know?
heap of rusty reflections, lie that smacks of truth: Being-there
with the rattle of inner thought, light refrain: I am
what I am; cow, sheep, lamb, dreamlike deer, snowy
stag from a poem that doubts: is there life behind the image?
snow's black sun I heard once, night's white
promontory; they're all lining up for the finale; my paradise
will have the same shades, same ideological intimations
(avoiding, as I always do, the cause) as this day that profits
shadows.

C

Menguante memoria, simbolista atributo de su río, aunque merodee,

aunque disminuya el caudal en porciones mezquinas y del agua

quede el chorro en cubeta, el surtidor en miniatura de azogue;

aunque se revele mera treta el aire, y desde un puro presente

sin historias, pura roca masticada por la sal, se restituya

su episodio humano, y la compasión de caras coincida

un instante con las palabras: he estado, he visto de nuevo,

en ese jardín, en esa casa, en esa calle, en ese barrio, en esa ciudad,

en ese país, y no peco de otro modo salvo interpretando: agua

de la superficie eres sentimiento de fondo, paloma de mí, cuervo

de la hora picoteando el hueco, oigo más: te quiero y no te quiero,

año arisco, paloma de mí o cuervo de la desidia, año discrepante,

fatalista, amedrentado, te quiero equívoco, vencido escollo

de metal, multitud gritona entre la turba de escamas,

no te quiero con el pico roto a la mitad, tu odio convertido

en una afición, cuervo, en mi río de agua hay más indulgencia

que espuma falsa, como aquel reborde ancho donde comienza

tu forma de isla, tu cisne de ti, aquel desvío terrenal donde blancamente

te eximo, leyendo siempre, la compasión a partir de una letra, agua,

sorna de los hechos, aquí nada pasa, se recuerda, nadie vive tanto

que no soporte callar, bruta imprecisión la del silencio, sus bestias

arrimadas al hombro, qué reclaman, nada, isla, no hubo tiempo

de ti ni trifulca en versión abstracta que te precediera; nada ocurre

con sentido, sino imita, isla, a tus demonios estridentes,

la caricatura de un descubrimiento:

C

Waning memory, symbolist attribute of its river, though it may prowl,
though the surge may drop off bit by bit until only the spurt of water
in the bucket remains, miniature jet of quicksilver;
though the air may reveal what amounts to a ruse, and from a storyless
pure present, pure rock chewed by salt, may restore
its human moment, and the compassion of faces may coincide
for an instant with words: I have been, I have seen once again, in
that garden, that house, that street, that neighborhood, that city,
that country, and have committed no sin but that of interpretation:
you, surface water, are deepest feeling, dove of mine, crow
of an hour pecking at hollows, I can hear more: I love and don't love you,
surly year, dove of mine or crow of apathy, year of discrepancies,
fatalism, alarm, I love you who are mistaken, battered metal
obstruction, shouting multitude mobbed by scales,
I don't love you with your beak broken in half, your hatred changed
into a hobby, crow, my river of water holds more indulgence
than false foam, like that wide ridge where the shape of your island
begins, your swan of yours, that earthly deflection where I give you
my pale pardon, reading, compassion from printed letters, water,
factual sarcasm, here nothing happens, is only remembered, no one
lives long enough to make silence unbearable, its wild imprecision,
its beasts at my shoulder, what's their demand, nothing, island, no time
for you, no abstract version of a brawl to precede you; nothing happens
with meaning, but only imitates, island, your strident demons,
caricature of a discovery:

D

Al revés no tendría la forma exacta, remolona, de la hermosura,

ni sería su opuesto, rumbo de más, estrafalario, la miga abstracta

en un sendero que bifurca su oriente hacia otra mezcla terrosa,

birlando el acueducto por un atajo yermo, surco de todos los surcos,

lastimando mi nítido concepto de río con su negro desagüe

en la colonia, callejón adentro, la historia de un niño a flote

hacia la pista del primer puente, fea desembocadura, latas

de diversa decadencia justo encima de un vórtice entre rocas

del agua siempre con su alambre, el cartón atorado entre papeles,

dónde iría ese remedo amarillo de un primer borboteo

bajo el sauce que libra su rastro en la luz, algo tan limpio,

el día de inicio, cosas aprendidas, en la cabeza el místico

gusano de una sola expectativa: que sea como dijeron, sea triste

al menos si no bello, escarcha en el aire, cochambre en los muros,

palomas de la piedra y tarde la ruina que oculta sus alusiones

a un estilo, ahí donde mi hermano en vida se jacta de haber visto

por el recodo, rémora del río, un cuerpo muerto y abultado,

se jacta de la miseria, casi fuera brillante, amoratada

mañana en los listones de pavimento donde busco jardín,

donde escuché huerto, andando entre baches hacia el vivero

más próximo, mi hermano, retenido el hábito de mirar

invisible, fuma tras el tronco salvaje, pino labrado en la ranura

entre la reja y el patio, fuma como yo debo hacerlo cuando pienso

que se me vino encima no el tiempo, vaya, que cualquiera

posee su clara filtración, sino la ironía de haberlo previsto

desde la quietud, sabiendo todo menos lo que pesa, la frase

por arriba de los hechos, preciso vaivén de palabras, pinta blanco

mi hermano, vigila su sombra, deviene pureza, mira la zanja

en el vivero, no hay pez de lastre, hoy carezco de animal amuleto,

D

Flowing backwards it would not have the exact, lazy shape of loveliness,

nor its opposite, too many ways to go, outlandish, abstract bead of

liquid on a path that forks east toward another earthy mixture,

taking a barren shortcut to swipe the aqueduct, furrow of all furrows,

wounding my clear-cut concept of river with its black seepage

in the suburbs, in the alleys, story of a young boy floating

into sight of the first bridge, river's ugly mouth, tin cans

in various stages of decay atop the rocky vortex,

water again with its barbed wire, cardboard fetched up against papers,

where would it go, that yellow mimicry of a first gurgle

under the willow that frees its trace to the light, something so clean,

the first day, lessons learned, in my head the mystic

worm of a single expectation: that it would be like they said, would

at least be sad, if not beautiful, hoarfrost in the air, filth on the walls,

stone doves and the late ruin that hides its allusions to a certain

style, over there where my living brother boasts of having seen,

just around the bend, blocking the river, a bloated corpse,

boasts of misery, almost brilliant, morning

black and blue on the ribbons of pavement where I seek a garden,

where I heard an orchard, walking the potholes toward the nearest

grove, my brother, retaining his role as invisible

watcher, smokes behind the wild trunk, wrought pine in the groove

between fence and yard, smokes like I must when I think

about what's come crashing down, not time, no, anyone

can hold its clear filtration, but instead the irony of having foreseen it all

in stillness, knowing everything except its weight, phrase

before facts, words' precise wavering, my brother paints it white,

watches over his shadow, becomes purity, looks at the ditch

in the grove, no fish for ballast, and me without my totem animal,

tanto rito de ignorancia entre paisajes que deambulan sueltos

por la pantalla con voces traducidas, mi león mermado,

mi tigre rutinario, yo no soy testigo, no tengo más piedad

que aquel vecino, aquel fulano, aunque se trate finalmente

de eso, empatía o amor, no siento en la punta de la lengua

incluso su efímera pitanza, donde vivo se daría como limosna

sentir por otro, ponerse en su lugar, pero persiste, hermano,

afuera, sí hay piadosas, agrietadas losetas que van dirimiendo

ángulos, afuera donde vivo, un hermano esconde a otro hermano,

hay hermosa lumbre, densos derrames por la pared al alba,

conozco esa luz dividida, mi iracundo destello por los colores

que no corresponden, virtudes de la bruma química,

mi conciencia lo sabe, no siente lo que es alba, hora de antes,

su máquina pospuesta, espíritu es lo que pongo

porque contradicho rinde y no concuerda

fabricando en orden su trampa.

such rites of ignorance among landscapes wandering loose

on the screen with dubbed voices, my diminished lion,

my everyday tiger, I'm no witness, have no more pity

than that neighbor, that no-name, even if that's what it's all about

in the end, empathy or love, I can't even taste their daily bread,

ephemeral on the tip of my tongue, in my world to feel for another,

to put myself in their shoes, is akin to giving alms, but it persists,

brother, out there where the merciful, rifted tiles slowly nullify

angles, out there in my world, one brother hides another brother,

a dense and lovely flame spills over the wall at dawn,

I know that divided light, my irate glimmer among clashing

colors, courtesy of the chemical haze,

my consciousness knows this, does not feel the dawn, an hour before,

its machine postponed, spirit is what I bring here

because it surrenders to contradiction and will not conform

setting its traps in place.

E

He andado por estos caminos;
los he imaginado vivos.

—Ezra Pound

Provincia desierta, margen de un arroyo laminado y lila, agua

que va al oeste, agua en ruta, he visto poco, hoy tiendo

a imaginar lo que habría sido con otra historia, no yo, puro sur

del sol en astillas, como si de un fuego naciera la peculiar

tradición de contemplarse por dentro, fulgor de paja, pavesa

de un alma despuntado, me tritura la convicción de haberla

espiado con burla, ¿eres alma o niebla?, distante velo, nube

cíclica de un olor, husmeo, hay alguien, toco, nadie

se extiende hasta mi extremo, alma no tiene voz, adentro huye,

mi fetiche de atributos, eres y soy, cuánto arte en el ocultamiento,

debajo la alegoría se destripa, mata metáforas, agua di

que no se asemeja a nada en su flujo cotidiano, ¿me tritura qué?

cualquier certeza es prejuicio, luego dónde se coloca aquella tibia

latitud, lo real mismo, defínelo, hermano, qué barrio de preferencia,

cuál nombre, qué trabajo, burocracia o teatro, vicio de entraña,

condenar prójimo, jueces de mí, tengo baraja, escondo reina,

puro rey hasta donde dure este descarrío, fealdad que aspira

a la hermosura, mi poste gris de halo insignificante, mi costra de luz

en la calle, qué bicho desata su guerra en el círculo de claroscuros,

fisura en medio, rastrero linde con el aceite de un coche, desastre

cuando hay trinchera en vez de gente, muro contencioso

contra solitarios, hermano engaña cuando hace falta, no soy

como soy, dice, historia de puro sur que divaga, moralmente

defectuosa quién quiere la verdad, si es odio cómo se proclama

sin lastimar el código colectivo, odio el mal, por ejemplo,

E

I have walked over these roads;
I have thought of them living.
—Ezra Pound

Provincia deserta, banks of an oily, lilac-swirling stream, water

runs west, water runs, I haven't seen much, these days I tend

to imagine who I might have been in someone else's story, not me,

sheer southern sun in splinters, as if the peculiar tradition

of self-contemplation were born of fire, glowing straw, ember

of a dawning soul, I'm crushed by the conviction that I've

spied on it in jest, are you soul or fog?, distant veil, scent's cyclical

cloud, I sniff, someone's there, I touch, no one

stretches toward my extremity, soul has no voice, flees within,

my fetish of attributes, you are, I am, such artful hiding,

the allegory underneath spills its guts, murders metaphors, water, say

that this daily flow resembles nothing else, I'm crushed by what?

every certainty is a prejudice, then where do we place that warm

latitude, the real itself, define it, brother, what favored neighborhood,

what name, what job, bureaucracy or theater, cherished vice,

condemn thy neighbor, judges of mine, I hold the cards, I hide the queen,

merely the king as long as this madness lasts, ugliness aspiring

to beauty, my gray post with its trifling halo, my crust of light

on the street, what gnat lets slip its war within the chiaroscuro circle,

cracked down the middle, creeps toward the puddle of motor oil,

disaster when you look for people and find a trench, a wall litigating

against the lonely, brother misleads when it's needed, I am not

what I am, he says, stories of the sheer south he rambles, who wants

the truth if it's morally flawed, if it's hate then how to proclaim it

without wounding the collective code, hatred of evil, for example,

sentimentalismo aparte, sería un deseo, pero el odio secreto,

esquinero, alma en piso, tierra, no lo anuncia nadie,

quién quiere saber, odio a un contrario, contrincante

que es amigo de alguien más, la cadena cómplice, mi eslabón

se atora donde redime a otro, quién quiere ser rabia ajena,

el grito afuera, adentro el placer de oírlo, cuánto lodo

entre cristal y calle, no es nada mi odio, hermano, te hundes,

más feo entonces el negro arroyo, el agua espesa,

por dónde, yegua bruta y tuerta, cabalgando hasta el símil

de un campo, inventa naturaleza, hocico, pezuña, rápido

antes de que duela, espina, lo que no se pudo ver a tiempo.

sentimentality aside, would be a desire, but that secret, cornered hate,

soul to the ground, to the earth, no one speaks of it,

who wants to hear it, hate thy enemy who is someone

else's friend, chain of conspirators, my link

jams as it frees another, who wants to be someone else's rage,

outside the shriek, inside the pleasure of hearing it, all that mud

between street and window, my hatred is nothing, brother, you take

the plunge, the black stream uglier then, the water thicker,

where does it go, wild one-eyed mare, galloping toward a simile

of countryside, inventing nature, muzzle, hoof, hurry

before it hurts you, thorn, spine, not seen in time.

F

Roto pabellón de un río, fugaz campaña de agua sucia,

agua destituida por la gula del aire, digo, codicia por el caudal

de fantasmas, mil caras de la basura, reitero, como si nadie

las hubiera visto, mil caras río abajo, la orilla simulada entre trozos

de hule, plásticos acarreados, un hilo que recorre los brotes,

río de las cosas, hacia dónde iba, te deslinda un idioma, te junta otro,

agua hincada en puro contrasentido, arcana agua ésta que se postula

como ánimo, habiendo tanto disfraz, mil caras son una sola,

mi hermano cuando llega usa la del mal, yo ninguna, rota la efigie

del inicio, vi formas no el sedimento donde a veces se anclaban,

cuéntame, pregunto lo mismo, hubo hierba donde creció la sombra,

pasto en la gruta, abrojo en la boca, lo mismo que muerdo, dónde

empezaron las frases atrofiadas por su belleza, mi hermano tuvo algunas,

el límpido filamento de un mar entre ojo y ojo, mirando el primer día,

lámpara occisa, la extinción simple de un objeto, foco desnudo

en el cielo raso, hermano ingenuo, pesimista por falta de astucia,

da vuelta la suerte, cuéntame, los mapas fortuitos de una cuadra,

el adoquín alterno para cada pie indeciso, la muletilla de una infancia

ubicua, cuéntala como si la creyeras, su vertiente invertida procrea

un leve jardín, casi cantado, un paraíso escrito sin discordia, hacia adentro,

hermano enemigo, el ídolo es aquel pasto o la dicha, canta y miente,

desde esa raya fronteriza donde hace agua la voz tan pronto se cuela

un dato, corrupto es quien pide o quien da, corrupta la merma

o la abundancia, lo mismo entonces, abusa de la imagen de ese fondo,

mil caras de un río retoman su secuela, muerdo lo que sé, datos

son tu barda son mi rueda son tu agua son mi calle, casa de otro polvo,

de otra estrofa, zanja derivada, declinante, raspadura del metal

contra la piel, óxido corrupto, episodio de un sepia trascendente,

imbuido de sí, hermano engasta, intuye mi fórmula de ríos empotrados,

F

River's broken pavilion, furtive campaign of dirty water,

water displaced by greedy air, I say, coveting the surge of ghosts,

garbage with a thousand faces, I repeat, as if observed by no one,

a thousand faces downriver, rubber tires forming a false bank,

plastic bottles carried along, a thread traversing the gush, river

of things, going where, one language sets you apart, one draws you in,

water plunged into contradiction, arcane water postulated as

a state of mind, so many disguises, a thousand faces a single face,

my brother arrives and tries on the face of evil, I refuse, the first effigy

broken, I saw shapes not the sediment they sometimes came to rest in,

tell me, I ask again, was there grass in the place where shadows grew,

grass in the grotto, thistle in the mouth, the one I bite, where did

the sentences stunted by their beauty begin, my brother spoke

a few, sea's limpid filament between the eyes, watching

the first day, defunct lamp, object simply snuffed out, bare bulb

in the cloudless sky, naïve brother, pessimistic from lack of cunning,

turn your luck around, tell me your story, fortunate maps of a city block,

a different cobblestone for each indecisive foot, catchphrase of a

ubiquitous childhood, as if you believe, its inverted pathway breeds

a delicate garden, almost a song, paradise written not lost, turning inward,

brother enemy, the idol is the grass, or else is joy, singing and telling lies,

on that borderline where the voice waters as soon as the facts

slip in, the asker as corrupt as the giver, corrupt in diminishment

or abundance, it's all one then, abusing the image of those depths,

the river's thousand faces resume their sequel, I bite back what I know, facts

are your wall my wheel your stream my street, house of a different

dust, a different stanza, channeled, dwindling ditch, metal scraping

skin, corrupted rust, moment of transcendent sepia, self-suffused,

brother embeds, intuits my formula of rivers made to order,

pabellones de viento o brisa cribada por la tela, inventa una verdad

que suene, cínicamente tenga la moldura del ruido antes del silencio,

paradoja del oído, llana verdad, templa de un extremo a otro

su agua relativa, nadie de oficio, hermano tendría que pasar

del retroceso de una conciencia al acto, escuetamente,

atravesar si no aquel espacio de terca prosodia, al menos

la franja de una luz que ocurra con el mundo adentro,

aunque mienta y diga que el reto desaparece tan pronto

se agota este ciclo de infierno, mi tramo de ocio desviado

hacia la eficiencia, mil caras de la cara única, juez de mí,

juez de ti, dictando paráfrasis, antecedentes de la fe más austera,

haya letanía, letargo en círculos que ciña al menos la circunstancia

de esta identidad sin dilema, agua del agua, yo tuve la idea

y la sentí antes de pensarla.

pavilions of wind or breeze sifted by cloth, invents a truth that rings,

cynically taking the form of the noise heard just before silence,

hearing's paradox, plain truth, tempers its relative water

from one end to the other, a nobody by trade, brother would have to pass

from retreating consciousness into action, crisply,

cross through if not that space of stubborn prosody, then at least

the band of light that occurs and the world within it,

even if I lie and say that the challenge disappears as soon as

this cycle of hell winds down, my leisure hours degenerate into

efficiency, single face with a thousand faces, judge of mine, of yours,

sentencing me to paraphrase, antecedents of the most austere faith,

let there be litany, lethargy circling, straitening at least the circumstance

of this unproblematic identity, water's water, it was my idea

and I felt it before I thought it.

G

Casi cantado el mundo por dentro, casi jardín la llanura esquiva,
casi elemento su río trunco, su río redundante por abstracto,
su margen de hierba minada por la corriente, su tesitura
de agua ronca, agua compleja que lidia consigo a falta
de otro concepto, idea de inicio: quién la piensa cuando recurre
al instinto, la reacción por inercia, agua contra el paliativo del cielo,
cómo suena, qué sueña cuando se abre en la percepción más inmediata
una fractura entre las horas, se introduce, por descuido, esa historia
alternativa, ese río en otra parte, lo mismo contrahecho que perfectible,
dando de sí, río de quien lo piense, de quien lo escuche, agua de ti
imaginando un instante tu cara en otra cara, la anécdota de alguna
persona primeriza, su cuento por lo bajo, persona prójimo,
puro oficio de gente: se despoje la horma, nada ceda porque nada
contiene mi adivinanza menor, treta de muchedumbre, tantas
cabezas por calle que conservan algún sentido, aunque yo lo calcule
en engaño por cuadra, desidia de la moral más simple, ese respeto
por semejanza, agua es lago es río es océano, es tú en esencia,
predicamento, lo que busco aunque sea remota la pesquisa,
ande yo por la calle como si fuera el mundo, no lo examine,
desconozca dónde comienza, alguna vez un día, oyendo, cascada
en cierne, credo de roca indistinta, o mirando la luz manantial,
su lumbre de hueco, su borde más antiguo donde no hay ninguno,
o descubra, entre la naturaleza especulativa, espejo primitivo,
un argumento de orden, cosas antes que palabras, jardín
en lugar de la página descrita, patio antes que esa conjugación
que retiene los sucesos para concederles el tiempo estrecho
de una frase, sombra de mi sombra, pida entonces menos
con mano ajena, tanto trino enturbia esa máscara de pájaro,
postizo pico que casi canta en el cable, se agosta en la cuerda,

G

Almost a song the world within, almost a garden the evasive plain,
almost an element its maimed river, its river redundant in abstraction,
its grassy banks cut away by the current, nuanced by rough
water, complex water battling itself for lack
of a better idea, a beginning: who thinks of water when resorting
to instinct, inertial reaction, water against the sky's balm,
how does it sound, what does it dream when the hours fracture
inside our immediate perception, carelessly introducing that other
story, that elsewhere river, at once misshapen and capable of perfection,
giving of itself, river belongs to the one who thinks it, hears it, water
of yours imagining your face in another's face, anecdote of a
barely fashioned person, a whispered secret, a person, an other,
merely a person: even if the form is stripped away, if nothing yields
because nothing contains my weakest guess, the crowd's ruse, all those
heads out there on the street making sense, even if I calculate
the betrayal block by block, a slovenly, simple morality, that respect
for likeness, water is lake is river is ocean, is you in essence,
predicament, is what I seek even in remote investigation,
even if I walk the streets as if they were the world, don't examine it,
don't understand where it starts, sometime someday, listening, sifting
the waterfall, blurred and rocky credo, or watching the spring-fed light,
its hollow flame, its oldest edge where no edge exists,
or even if I discover, in nature's speculation, primitive mirror,
an idea of order, things before words, garden
instead of written page, backyard before the conjugation
that quells events to proffer them the narrowed space
of a sentence, my shadow's shadow, even if I ask for less
with another person's hand, so much warbling muddying the bird mask,
false beak almost singing on the cable, parched on the wire, even if I

sea barroca, o clame desde el hoyo en medio de un techo
sin gamas, puro techo del mundo adentro, por las cosas ordinarias,
otra dicción con la multitud a su alcance y, siendo sabia, disimule.

am baroque, or cry out from the hole in the center of a colorless
roof, merely the roof of the world within, for ordinary things, for a
language with the multitudes at hand and even if, wisely, I pretend.

H

Meditemos que el silencio
se asemeja al esqueleto
de una teoría...
—Jorge Hernández Campos

Uña de mi luna, te llamo por artificio, leve paso de luna, leve vida,
maña de este tramo, define lo que dura, aire si es aire, hermano
de otro infierno, aire que va y viene hoy en el día, los demonios idénticos
de esta mañana, uno que gasta la premisa de su bondad en la compasión
que siente: pobre mundo, susurra, pobre, tres veces pobre por negarme;
otro, tú y yo por encima: cálido demonio, vigilante y sometido a mi duda,
tiempo de pensar, me sugiere, tiempo de mirar hacia fuera donde cunde
mi mundo, pobre diatriba de diablo, me digo, posesivo con su gente
    ese diablo
que cae un martes de marzo, diablo sin el rumor de la población agitada;
argumento mío: orden que proviene de palabras será de superficie,
aunque por dentro, sigiloso remedo, evolucione hacia la sencillez
de un destino bellamente delineado, feo en su fondo, prescribe la regla;
diablo vagabundo, diablo quieto, qué discierno, un río que me habla
desde el circuito de su agua en mi cabeza como si leyera: colmena
en el infierno, cuál zumbido cierra, diablo, el camino hacia la muerte,
cuál subterfugio, ceniza de un verano ordinario o el truco de la miel misma,
dulzura a cambio de inocencia, aunque no soy yo quien la pide, es del
    diablo
la demora, es la luna que divaga, mi fósil luna en este cielo, lugareña luna,
quién te clava, cierta un día cualquiera, quién predice el odio a veces, luna
inexacta en otro espejo, luna hilada por un ojo de agua, calculo tu enredo,
eres sonido que no se ve, eres mi ciego diablo, traspié del río en la curva,
tartamudo río, lengua de tu agua, dónde termina la ficción, empieza

H

Let us consider that silence
resembles the skeleton
of a theory...
—Jorge Hernández Campos

Spoon of my moon, I call you with all my guile, moon's light step, light life,
skilled stretch that defines what lasts, air and only air, brother
from another hell, air that comes and goes in daylight, this morning's
identical demons, one who wastes his premised kindness on the compassion
he feels: poor world, he whispers, poor thing, thrice as poor to deny me;
another, with us atop: kindly, watchful, submitting to my doubt,
time to think, he suggests to me, time to look outside where my world
looms, poor devil diatribe, I tell myself, so possessive of his people,
    that devil who falls on a Tuesday
in March, devil missing the murmurs of an agitated populace;
my train of thought: any order derived from language is superficial,
although within, stealthy mimicry, it may evolve into the simplicity
of a destiny beautifully outlined but ugly at bottom, as prescribed by rule;
vagabond devil, hushed devil, what do I discern, a river that talks to me
from water's circuit in my head as if reading: hell's
beehive, what sort of buzzing, devil, slams the door on death,
what subterfuge, ashes of an ordinary summer or honeyed trick,
sweetness exchanged for innocence, though I'm not the one who's
    asking, it's the devil's delay,
it's the moon's digression, my fossilized moon in this sky, local moon,
who stabbed you, on any given day, who predicts hatred, faulty moon
in another mirror, threaded by a spring, I calculate your entanglement,
you're a sound unseen, my blind devil, river's stumble on the curve,
stuttering, water of your tongue, where does fiction end and

el recuerdo preconcebido por mi pregunta, qué desciende, diablo,

qué espiral sin alma se retuerce en otra fórmula del tiempo,

qué demonio fuera de tu ley, refugio de tu broma, grita suelo

cuando apenas tanteo el aire, cuál luna me adjudica este silencio

que desperdicio evocando algún sustituto menor en cada aspa

de la luz, no soy yo, quién lo pide, culpa de la memoria, automatismo

que pasa por ser conciencia, sosiego que se rememora, no se escucha,

diablo maldito, hábito del aire, te tiento amigo, te tiento risa, no

    hubo sensible,

ambiguo cielo en la esfera máxima, mente sin orillas, conociéndose,

luna adentro, tan temida la sorpresa de no hallar a nadie tras el esqueleto,

ninguna persona peleada con las nociones de un nombre, áspera rima

sin dilema, tedio no se abstiene, simple la manivela del diablo enciende

su hora, la sopesa, nada obstruye esta racha, luna crónica, diablo

no piensa, compara mundo con mundo, látigo de su cola, agudamente,

fue mejor el final que el principio.

memory begin, preconceived in my question, what descends, devil,

what soulless spiral twists in another of time's formulas,

what demon outside your law, in the shelter of your joke, shouts land

when I'm barely fumbling for air, what moon allots this silence

that I waste evoking a lesser substitute with every beam

of light, it's not me, who's asking?, memory's guilt, automatism

passed off as consciousness, remembered calm, never heard,

damned devil, air's habit, I tempt you friend, tempt you laughter,

    there was no sensitive,

ambiguous heaven in the highest sphere, shoreless mind, self-knowledge,

moon within, fearful surprise of finding no one behind the skeleton,

no person at war with the notion of a name, rough and unproblematic

rhyme, boredom never abstains, devil's simple crank starts up its hour,

tests its weight, nothing impedes this streak of luck, chronic moon,

devil doesn't think, compares world to world, sharply whips his tail,

ends better than he began.

I
_____

Si comienzo: cuál tiniebla, belfo hundido por el fango, cuál golpe de agua

cuando truena contra su borde quisquilloso qué yegua muerta, dónde,

simulacro de batalla, cuál molde de una derrota apenas advertida precede

esta contienda entre bestias, este cálculo de rutinas a mitad de un

sentimiento;

o declaro, fuera máscara, hermano, te proscribo, tanto pones la mejilla,

resoplas, confundes honor con prudencia, y nada sabes de sangres,

ninguna tiñe tus destellos, lúcido hermano de alma magra, cómo vino

este animal a ser tu alegoría, cómo muerto te transcribe, mete diablo

donde sólo medra el oleaje tímido de ese riachuelo concurrido por el mosco

y el tornasol de un lubricante, chapoteo entre el sucio enigma de un agua

que cancela reflejos y muda su solipsismo hacia el centro, lo oigo,

cuánto concepto te posterga, habla oblicuo de ti, hermano, la ternura

tendrá su propio espejismo, amará lo que se escapa, nunca el cuerpo asible,

sino su huida, yegua de calle, crin abstracta, qué toco en la zona bermeja,

qué quiebro contigo, hermano, la forma de mi estancia, su vidrio sarcasmo,

su verde vista que columbra lo obvio, lo sustantiva, confunde orgullo

con inteligencia, se mofa de tanto sol secundario, nunca vio la idea,

sólo la usura de su brillo, puritana dicta, esto no fue, la silla me posa,

la mesa me inclina, no conoce salvo si describe, estrecha, pero hubo

mente

más allá del dato, fuera oscuro, hubo hueso, política de friso, aquí se vende,

aquí se ofrece, dádiva o recompensa, nunca percibió el cariz, vía

cadáver,

vía ley postergada hasta la comedia, indignamente común para los

sentidos,

valga el rigor de cualquier hipótesis, carcajada hasta la caída del telón,

adónde voy, mi hermano de casa, mi hermano colectivo, ignoro el dialecto

de las buenas costumbres, muertos que matan muertos tienden a

I

If I begin: what kind of darkness, muzzle engulfed by mud, what wall
of water slams what dead horse against its finical bank, and where,
mock battle, what empty mold for a barely expected defeat precedes
this strife between beasts, this calculation of routines midway through
    a feeling; or do I declare,
down with the mask, brother, away with you, always turning your cheek,
snorting, taking honor for prudence, you know nothing of blood,
it never stains your rays, lucid lean-souled brother, how did this animal
come to be your allegory, how does its death transcribe you, insert a devil
where all that thrives is the timid swell of a stream upon which mosquitoes
and iridescent oil converge, splashing in the dirty enigma of a water
that voids reflection and moves its solipsism toward the center, I hear it,
concepts postpone you, talk around you, brother, tenderness
makes its own mirage, loves what slips away, never the body safe in arms
but only its escape, street mare, abstract mane, what do I touch in the
red zone, what do I break with you, brother, the shape of my time with
    you, its glass sarcasm,
its green vision taking in the obvious, nominalizing it, confusing pride
with intelligence, scoffing at so much secondary sun, never seeing the idea,
only the usury of its gleam, puritanical dictum, none of this took place,
the chair seats me, the table bends me, knows nothing except in
    description, narrowing, but did the mind
exist beyond the facts, was it dark, were there bones, a politics
of ornament, for sale, for free, gift or compensation, never seeing how it
    was, by way of the corpse,
by way of a law laughably postponed, shamefully common to the senses,
so much for the accuracy of any hypothesis, cackling until the curtain falls,
where am I going, my own brother, my collective brother, I don't
    speak the dialect

revivirlos,
por cordura o por ciencia, no condeno, es mi casta cínica la que me
sugiere
caballos de estante, cacharros difusos en aquella tiniebla donde atisbo
hermano a la vez que cómplice, aunque ya un tercero en discordia
se vaticine, comience, bala, bulto, se tenga en pie, vaya retiro,
para que nadie venga en paz.

of social graces, when the dead kill the dead they end up bringing
    them back to life,
by sense or science, I'm not judging, my cynical caste is what suggests
    to me
horses as props, trash dim in that darkness where I peel my eyes
for brother as well as accomplice, although a discordant third already
is foretold, begins, bullet, bulk, to keep its feet, to waive refuge,
so that no one comes in peace.

J

Levantar el misterio donde no le hay es helado
desaire, porque da en vacío la ponderación.

—Baltazar Gracián

Eh, tanta tentación de mundo, luz leonina que bebe agua de recoveco,
desconoce el hoyo mal descrito o en qué persona regreso, mi fardo
de vuelta, no lo tengo sino en origen, en objeto de intemperie, caliza
ladera que no existe salvo si la percibo, cautivo en cierta frase,
mi hermano más simple, dónde pondré este día, su mezquino polvo
en alguna parte, su caridad vicaria, dónde soy afuera, ni quién diga
con qué coyuntura, buena causa, debe ensalzarse mi lástima,
ni por qué leyendo pierdo la forma del juego, recalco sin experiencia
los hechos, leyendo como si yo tuviera la razón sólo por entender
las palabras, medir sutilezas entre líneas, fijando el castigo por tanto
paisaje falso, que hice yo, pero extendiste tú, hermano de umbral,
dispersamente, esos colores que no corresponden, columna de ti
tan rota por su rojo, por su azul, nadie en su sano juicio comulgaría
con esa claridad, la trunca ley del matiz no sabe nada empíricamente,
se evade por un atajo, mítica pericia, vistiendo dioses, pandemonio,
hubo un bosque donde hoy se atasca el alambre con su propia herrumbre,
falso, mi hermano melancólico, devoto de un antes impoluto, en toda fecha
se extraña la anterior, come de sí su retrato, su inmerso parásito de tan
    breve
utopía, cara de un agua en el agua, pondera, no diré el nombre, saña
de la multitud que pide derroteros cuando apenas deambulan por esa
    ladera
una opinión tras otra, pastan cuando hay dónde, pobre símbolo, vaca
    enjuta
de lo que pienso, librada la brecha, la seca planicie, ningún lugar persiste

J

To raise up mystery where none exists is a frozen
and graceless act, because it produces only emptiness.
—Baltazar Gracián

Ah, how the world tempts us, leonine light drinking from the streamlet,

unaware of the poorly described hole or in what person I return, bringing

my burden back, just what I began with, an object unsheltered, chalky

hill that doesn't exist until I perceive it, captive in a certain phrase,

my simplest brother, where do I place this day, its measly dust,

its vicarious charity, where do I place my being outside, who decides

upon what occasion, good cause, my pity should be praised, or why

when I read do I lose hold of the game, foreground the facts without

experience, reading as if I've got it right just because I understand the
    words,

weighing subtleties between the lines, settling on a punishment for this

false landscape, I made it, but you took it further, threshold brother,

diffusely, all of those clashing colors, column of yours so broken

by its red, by its blue, no one in their right mind would commune

with that clarity, the maimed law of intimation knows nothing empirically,

finds a shortcut, mythical prowess, dressing the gods, pandemonium,

once there was a forest where today the barbed wire chokes on its
    own rust,

false, my melancholy brother, devotee of an unpolluted past,

always longing for yesterday, eating away at its portrait, its submerged
    parasite of briefest

utopia, water's face in the water, give it weight, I won't say the name, fury

of the multitude that demands a destination when they're barely wandering
    the hillside

one opinion after another, pasturing where they may, paltry symbol,

más allá, diremos, de la beata monarquía de mis ojos, que algo buscan
  salvar,
algún mendrugo, mi hermano en dislate, bajando por aquel camino
que no retocaré, fea tangente de basura, la materia es lo inefable,
la verdad que no se derruye, pues ni quién venga luego a levantar
cadáver, si hay tanta luz de boca que lo persigue y ni hueso que
  sobreviva
de su secreto, desaire de la oreja, ya lo filtre mi turba, ya incurra
en mí su dilatada serie, número negro, va mi león arrastrándolo
como si fuera carnaza, lo punza con su colmillo, por dentro halle sol,
encarne un instante, mate su cuerpo vivo, y a quien lo añada, otra vez,
mi animal de paso ande desmenuzando el intento, ande desgarrando
  la teoría.

bony cow

of what I think, unimpeded gap, dry plain, no place persists beyond,

shall we say, the blessed monarchy of my eyes, searching for something
    to save,

some crust of bread, my senseless brother, descending on that road

I refuse to retouch, ugly tangent of garbage, matter is ineffable,

an indestructible truth, and anyway who would want to expose

a corpse, when so much of the mouth's light pursues it and not even
    a bone to survive its secret,

ear's gracelessness, let it be filtered by my mob, let its prolonged

series incur in me, black number, there goes my lion dragging it

like bait, piercing it with sharp teeth, will it expose the sun within,

incarnate an instant, kill the living body, and as for the one who would
    add to it,

once more, will my animal pass through to dismantle the attempt, to
    rip the theory apart.

K

Cómo siempre asoma el guarismo
bajo la línea de todo avatar.
—César Vallejo

Postizo santo, mi santo, mi calle de rata y yeso, mi coartada de mosaicos
imaginados entre las vetas de un oro difícilmente atribuible a la especie,
oro de un aire contrario al oro mismo, oro de nadie, mi refranero giro:
otra vez no sé lo que sé, el caduco tronco, la vacua madera que retengo
cuando me construyo, astilla de mí, no de nuevo, salta el perno a la vista,
sin herramienta me pospongo, pausa de mí oyendo la estructura,
la calle misma donde se pule un ruido tan faccioso como su idea,
se mina la cauta visión, cuánto parque, procedimiento de parque,
principio de realidad, va desplazando el árbol hacia su arquetipo
cuando no se tiene en reserva alguna historia, no se mete mundo
donde hay cabida, hermano reticente, mi estribillo te jala, todo pasado
sea copia de muerte, carta gastada, habrá corredor para la fila extensa,
amigos y enemigos, jueces absueltos de ti, de mí, incluso quien narre,
obsesivo, ciudad o persona, nada importa, tanto se disgregan ambas
cuando se cuentan entre los vivos, ingeniosamente, vaya siendo
cierta mi luida emoción, mi ínsula entonces de arcos esbeltos, mi clima
lento como el vapor que apenas se desprende de la huella húmeda
sobre el asfalto, pie hundido en un sol entero, bajo esa primavera
pendiente, manipuladora, nunca sea hermosa la violeta jaspeada
por el hollín que se tuerce en un gris menor, dónde la cuelgo, narro
los inicios, naturaleza obliga, un mediodía sin retazos verbales
en que se inmiscuya el roedor testigo, mastique la falla, el pedazo
de cuerda suspendido hasta que vuelva a crearse una costa de moho
en su pozo, algún quiebre, agua menos asidua, te retomo en pista,
te pienso, agua, derrame limpio, por el oído te pienso, cancelo la casa

K

How always the cipher appears
under every avatar's line.
—César Vallejo (trans. Rebecca Seiferle)

Synthetic saint, my saint, my rat-and-plaster street, my alibi of imagined

mosaics among veins of a gold hardly to be recognized as such,

gold of an air that goes against gold, no one's gold, my habitual phrase:

once more I don't know what I know, leafless trunk, hollow wood left over

when I build myself, splinter of mine, not again, the bolt jumps out,

lacking the tools I postpone myself, pause of mine as I hear the structure,

the street itself where a sound is polished until it is as seditious as its idea,

undermining wary sight, look at the park, the park as process,

reality's onset, displacing the tree towards its archetype

when there's no story in reserve, no world inserted with room to hold it,

reticent brother, tugged by my refrain, the past is a duplicate of death,

a worthless card, there's hallway enough for the queue, friends and

    enemies,

blameless judges of yours, of mine, even the one who tells the story,

obsessive, city or person, it doesn't matter, since they both fall apart

here in the land of the living, ingenious, as if my threadbare emotion

could ever be true, my islet of slender curves, my climate

slow like the steam that barely rises from the wet print

on the asphalt, foot submerged in a whole sun, below that pending,

manipulative springtime, never so beautiful the violet streaked

by soot twisted in gray minor, where do I hang it, I tell of

beginnings, nature compels me, a noon without snippets of conversation

where the rodent witness could encroach, gnaw away the fault, the length

of rope left hanging until it comes to create a moldy coast

in its well, a breakage, less assiduous water, I overtake your trail,

donde vive la gente, iniciales de tres caras, mixta escritura

de un lado odiando, nunca por la ele, torpemente deduciendo

briznas de bizancio, escúchame, por tanto artificio, y más tarde,

casi noche, haciendo griego con las letras que sobran, haciendo mata

con el embrollo, pura gallina de aquí en adelante, santa gallina que

escarbe

lo que fue, señoras y señores, lo que es, su festín de baba sin temple

cuando se espuma hacia la ira, gallina antes de que a mí me agarre

el agua primera de alguna razón, hermano de mí, y a ti te estanque

en ese coto donde vengo a numerar plegarias por hoscos ritos,

por puertas cerradas, por castigo, pues dije, quién va por mí

siendo tú, hermano, el más inocente.

I think of you, water, clean sweep, I think of you with my ear, I negate
the house where the people live, initials with three faces, mixed writing,
hatred on the one hand, never through the letter, clumsily deducing
Byzantine blades of grass, listen to me, through all the artifice, and later,
nearly night, speaking Greek with the letters that are left, heaping up
the rubbish, nothing but chickens from here on out, sainted hen scratching
what was, ladies and gentlemen, what is, its unhinged banquet of slobber
as it foams into rage, chicken before reason's first water
grabs me, brother of mine, and confines you
to those grounds where I come to number supplications for sullen rites,
for closed doors, for punishment, like I said, who goes through me,
you being, brother, the innocent one.

L

Tuvo otra suerte, amalgamado a la solapa, ese trópico de pacotilla,

ese chasquido de metal en la tradicional boca, cuando por el trapecio

de los dientes se figuraba otro hito buscado, trópico de estraza,

metiendo papel en las junturas del alma, trópico de hebra irresuelta,

zurciendo las retículas de su mapa, hasta dónde iría, olvidando mi barrio

de aquel modo, el lugar donde anido chuscamente, ala de latón,

    asómate

niña, mi hermano hondo, asómense: hay repique de lianas contra

el barranco, hay zancudos adivinando si será sangre, seré yo la piel

ecuménica donde un aguijón horade su camino hacia el centro;

hay chango deletreando cuando hablo, mono utilitario, filológico mono

que agarro al vuelo, descuelgo del viento, y algo de garra se me queda

si ato las caras del mono a un gesto único de dolor plagiado, soy yo,

le repito al mono, esa mueca batida con la sorna, ese teatro a campo

traviesa, tramando con mi atril algún espíritu menos fechado, que

    no piense

en sí como si existiera por inercia nominativa, niña, detén la soga, hermano,

tantea esta atmósfera, casi el humo te aturde como una pared equidistante

entre tus dedos y mi festín de fantasmas, migajas del ánimo medianero,

tanto obstruye a mi trópico esa exuberancia de hojas, humus revuelto

con el tobillo que lo esculpe, caminando, tanto aquietan sus palmeras

los ojos más ajenos, palmeras en la calle por el delirio que se amansa

a tus espaldas, hermano correcto, escampa su testa con la sierpe

enrollada en un grito, chango de puro asombro, asciende uña

por la corteza, corre, niña, mi mono al hombro me susurra,

eres tiempo, toca, chango blando y frío, tirana claridad, se ve

igual que ayer, trópico de tañidos, acoge el tímpano,

atemperado, un distinto rumor ahí.

L

Its fate was otherwise, glommed onto the lapel, that tropic of rubbish,

that metal snapping in the traditional mouth, when the teeth's

trapeze suggested another looked-for landmark, tropic of rags,

newspapers stuffed in the soul's cracked joints, tropic of loose ends,

darning the grid lines on its map, how far would I go, forgetting my

neighborhood in that way, the place where I make my clumsy nest, tin

    wing, look here

daughter, my deep brother, look here: thick vines pealing against

the gully, mosquitoes sniffing out blood, and I, the ecumenical

skin where a needle bores its path towards the center; here is

the monkey spelling when I speak, utilitarian, philologist monkey

I catch on the fly, unclasp from the wind, and a paw is left to me

if I tie down the monkey's faces to one look of plagiarized pain, it's me,

I tell the monkey, that grimace shot with irony, that cross-country theater,

plotting at my lectern a less anachronistic spirit, one that doesn't think

its existence is due to nominative inertia, daughter, roll up the rope,

    brother,

fumble for this atmosphere, smoke nearly stuns you like a wall separating

your fingers from my banquet of ghosts, crumbs of a middling mood,

my tropic so deeply obstructed by that leafy exuberance, humus stirred

by the ankle that sculpts it, walking, its palm trees so deeply hush

all other eyes, palms on the street because of the delirium soothed

behind your back, courteous brother, cooling its head with the snake

coiled into a shout, monkey is all astonishment, ascends nail

on bark, run, daughter, monkey whispers over my shoulder,

you are time, touch here, icy soft monkey, tyrant clarity, it all

looks the same as yesterday, tropic of bells, the eardrum admits,

tempered, a different murmur there.

M

Traste viejo será el dinero en ese barrio de siempre, hermano de penas,

tan fructífera la mugre que discurre con su río en medio, antiguamente

bajo un verde madroño, habría que rectificar, cuáles cadencias se dis-

tinguen,

mi eme o astilla varada, cuando se detiene en su espejo súbito alguna pose

entre tanta honestidad, remilgo medieval o reformista, elige, amigo

de carroña erudita, quién eres, me rindo, bajo lupa tanto servicio al

poderoso

parecería vocación, lengua enredada, trátate como si fueras yo, rebuscando

pueblo donde asciende lumbre con himno, tizne en la tesitura, dígase a

tu paso,

finalmente, hubo utopía tras el último número, para los cuantos al menos,

y aunque yo no tuve la razón conservé la maquinaria devota del silencio,

quien no se pronunciara entonces fue lidiando introspectivamente con

la duda,

inútil la intimidad cuando ya no hay dueño que murmure a tu espalda:

eres mío, hermano de talla, amigo público, devélate en estatua aunque sea

un instante, mármol lastimoso ése que traes de muestra, cuánto se

inmiscuye

la circunstancia en tu lasca, hiende roca como si fuera carne posterior a

un acto

de clemencia, canónica la tira de cuerpo que arroja en la calle el que

gobierna

en código estético, larga su esdrújula, me mofo, gasto colores, se

promulgue

una regla para cada accidente, lengua hermanada con aquel requisito

de bondad, corral de mi gracia, ruede justicia en su pocilga, sería prueba

de poco ingenio, aunque vayan los buenos sentimientos en clave

por la banqueta, amigo o dueño, se resienta la tradición en la rasposa acera

M

Money comes cheap as dirt in that old neighborhood, brother of sorrows,
so fruitful the filth flowing around its river, long ago
under a green arbutus, this must be rectified, which rhythms stand out,
my M or splinter run aground, when in its sudden mirror affectation pauses
amidst the honesty, a medieval or reformist scruple, your choice,
friend of erudite carrion, who are you, I surrender, under the loupe
    such service to the powerful
would seem to be a vocation, tongue-tied, do unto yourself as you
    would unto me, searching out
a town where flame rises with a hymn, smudged nuance, let it be said
    when you appear,
finally, utopia hid behind the last number, at least for some,
though I was wrong I preserved the devout machinery of silence,
she who would not declare herself was waging an introspective war
    with doubt,
intimacy is useless without the master murmuring at your back:
you're mine, brotherly sculpture, public friend, unveil your statue if only
for an instant, pitiful marble you display to others, watch how circumstance
    encroaches
while you chip away, cleaves rock as if it were flesh following an act
of mercy, canonical the corpses piled in the street by someone who
    governs
with aesthetic discipline, that lengthy dactyl, I'm just joking, I use all
    the colors, perhaps
a rule is enacted for every accident, tongue twinned with the obligation
of kindness, my grace corralled, let justice roll in its hole, this would prove
you lack wit, even if good intentions travel encoded on the sidewalk,
friend or master, tradition falls to pieces on the rough pavement
where what is humanly possible is besmirched for the first time

donde se embarra por primera vez lo humanamente posible con un quiebre

entre la coladera y agua de más, negra virtud circular que huye por la zanja,

tantas veces pillada en esa sustancia implícita, sea por mano mía, harapo

discreto haciendo de muñón donde no alcanzan los dedos para la

plegaria

que desconoce rutinas, pero ásperamente las convoca, como si fuera

alguien,

enseñando desde aquí algunos rastros de benevolencia mundana: ese muro

descendiente, ese faro proscrito por la curva; ilumíname, amigo de

salmos

breves en la glorieta que circunda, cantarino cobre, callado plástico, eres

lo que eres, según la arcaica cláusula, primero agua, cauce bíblico, mi

hermano

de propiedades, vándala estaca reclamando su frontera, puño en la reja,

es lo mismo el aullido que las palabras dispuestas en orden cuando se

gritan,

desdicen al dueño, dinero mata susurros, certezas de moneda esos

atisbos

de paisaje que enumero en segunda, vacilando, pedestre árbol, indico,

castigado por la bajeza del cielo, observo, algo moral que se desdeña

en el tronco ni se menciona, mi amigo de veleidades, te postulo

por costumbre, que si yo tuviera la misma memoria sería surco

de mí, proyecto de un buen recuerdo, prístina en retrospectiva,

rememorando conceptos como si construyera objetos.

with a break

between drain and overflow, black circular virtue fleeing into the ditch,

captured so many times in that implicit substance, even if by my hand,

discreet rag used as a stump where fingers cannot reach for the

supplication

that ignores routines, but abruptly summons them, as if it were someone,

demonstrating from here some trace of worldly benevolence: that

sloping

wall, that lighthouse banished by the curve; enlighten me, friend of brief

psalms on the encircling roundabout, singing copper, silent plastic, you are

what you are, so says the archaic dictum, first there was water,

biblical course, my propertied

brother, Vandal stake laying claim to its borders, fist on the fencepost,

a howl is the same as words arranged in perfect order when they are

shouted,

are unworthy of their master, money kills whispers, easy currency in

those hints

of landscape I enumerate in second person, hesitating, ordinary tree, I

indicate,

punished by lowly sky, I observe, something moral scorned

along the trunk isn't even mentioned, my fickle friend, I propose you

as is my custom, if I had the same power of recollection it would be

a furrow of myself, project of a happy memory, pristine in hindsight,

recalling concepts as if constructing objects.

N

Perplejo, ¿eres tábano de la mente?, o quién piensa derivando

en islas súbitas tanta arena de balde para definir la tierra, repartiendo

en litorales que se esfuman tan pronto se dejan de imaginar, mares rotos

por la esquina, divididos por un escaño de vidrio, de costa infrecuente,

de pata rala por la espuma hasta donde va creciendo otra alternativa,

qué tábano o yo taimado concibe una fe tan fiera, tras bambalinas,

fe de hilo y golpe de leño, moviendo el títere de un sentido como si fuera

divina la voluntad cuando se inmiscuye con una materia áspera, crujiente,

títere del baile analógico, tumbado en el piso, mi tábano mismo en la veta,

tábano de un titubeo, qué daría por la certidumbre, mi brinco de pies

bajo la corona de un cielo diminuto, calcando el vals más figurativo,

por aquí, ronda de encajes, por aquí, zapatillas en vez de fuego milenario,

la punta hacia arriba, hasta donde indique este viraje caviloso, reseco fulgor,

me diga que hay prenda a cambio, patines pospuestos hasta comprobar

que debajo de la mente se despliegue el hielo más lúcido de la duda,

linde con el juego, inmóvil tábano por dentro de la cabeza, y yo mire

mundo y barrio intermitente como un doblaje extenso, palabra por palabra,

hermano entre hermanos, de esa broma incierta, rimando *dé* con *Lyonnais*,

cántaro casi al borde mío, se avenga el títere en recaída, remede a mitad

de una frase ríspida o rancia, depende: ¿te conozco o me conozco?, tábano

engañoso, no hay nadie cuando veo el obelisco de luz en la grava de mi día

inmediato, circunstancial, ni cuando desaparece, llama extinta, tras la hilera

civil que recorre las calles siempre con propósito, adónde esta vez, si

    me dijeras,

enamorado de una voz auricular, tábano del viento oscuro, de la noche

    paralela,

por qué adjetivas una sensación, podría yo resignarme, culpa

por culpa pagada, ¿amas, o sólo posees lo que callas?, paradoja mediante,

mi hermano taciturno, hay justo que se arrepiente, voz tuya si la sueño

N

Perplexed one, are you the mind's gadfly?, or who is thinking, diverting
buckets of sand into sudden islands to define the earth, distributed
into littorals that vanish when they cease to be imagined, seas with
shattered corners, divided by a glassy seat, a seldom shore, a shank
combed by foam to the place where another alternative grows,
what gadfly or sly self conceives of a faith so fierce, behind the curtain,
a faith in strings and wood, moving the puppet in one direction as if
divine will encroaches on a rough, creaking surface,
puppet dances an analogy, falls to the floor, my gadfly in the grain,
giddy gadfly, what would I give for certainty, my feet skipping
beneath the crown of a tiny sky, tracing the most figurative waltz,
over here, whirl of lace, over here, satin slippers instead of millennial fire,
pointing upwards, wherever this neurotic twirling leads, this arid glow,
offering me security, laying the skates aside until it's confirmed
that doubt's most lucid ice unfolds beneath my mind,
bordering on a game, motionless gadfly inside my head, and if I watch
world and neighborhood flash on and off as if fully dubbing, word for word,
brother among brothers, that dubious joke, rhyming *day* with *Lyonnais*,
water-jar almost at my edge, if the puppet resolves on relapse, mimics
a sentence sharp or spoiled, it depends: do I know you or do I know
     myself?, deceitful
gadfly, no one is there when I see light's obelisk on the gravel of my
immediate, circumstantial day, or when it disappears, extinguished
     flame, behind the line of police
traversing the streets, ever purposeful, where to this time, if you told me,
loving an auricular voice, gadfly of dark winds, of parallel night,
why you turn a feeling into an adjective, could I resign myself, guilt paid by
guilt, do you love or only possess what you keep quiet?, in paradox,
my taciturn brother, a righteous person repents, your voice if I dream it

antes de la mañana, resonando como un cable inserto en mi quilla,

la tengo propuesta, mi impune quilla, me repito, traiciona cualquier

imperativo, tábano con tu mar de lona bailando, para qué escrutas,

repelas si hay albedrío, voz que pregunta: ¿andas ahí, del otro lado,

eres tú, tábano de mi cálculo, o quién medra escéptico de ti a mí

como si yo no quisiera conservarte en la cabeza, mi alguien predilecto,

zumbido de persona o partero anticuado de mi más remota idea?

before morning, reverberating like a wire thrust into my keel,

I propose, my unpunished keel, I repeat, it betrays every

imperative, gadfly with your sea of dancing sails, why do you scrutinize,

catechize free will, voice that asks: are you there, on the other side,

is that you, gadfly of my calculation, or whose skepticism thrives in us

as if I didn't want to keep you here in my head, my sweet someone,

buzzing of a person or antiquated midwife of my most remote idea?

Ñ

y la costumbre grecolatina de mentir
—Gerardo Deniz

Tanto distrae esa barbarie con su mula secular, su rama de valle muerto,
bajando por un flanco hacia ti, hermano transitorio, dando pezuña por arte,
mandíbulas restituidas a su dominio por la paja, un escupitajo al borde
de cualquier experiencia, como aquella mínima, talachera de una luz filtrada
por la multitud que acusa, púrgate con aire, pide, hambre antes que ideas
en este camino yerto donde le va cediendo la conciencia su lugar inocuo
a la miseria, azarosa teoría, cuál escritura te pretende, hermano solidario,
cacofonía al margen, tajada o a raja tabla, quién decide, ningún ruido
sin antes cerciorarme, sondeando huecos, de que aquí merodeó con cierta
ansia la mansedumbre, su espalda curva de hueso blando, la sensatez
en calidad de limosna, y lo que rocé entonces, hermano culto, en esa piel
que era de otro, prójimo si quieres, no hermano sino visitante, aspaviento
en el corazón, fue su vida como un comienzo, primera tripa sin entonar,
sonando por esa piel no obstante, o rechinando, vaya sol salvaje,
como si midiera su retroceso en minutos de timbre agudo por el filo
que alumbraría su metal, mula retórica, quién me despoja de la ventaja,
pienso mientras miro, yendo por tu lomo yo ficticia a contrapelo,
quién le da la vuelta al sentido, cavilo, cabeza quejumbrosa la que designa
fórmulas, simple se bifurca, dando culebra doble por recta vía, algo
que duele se entiende, repta, mula que va y viene en laberinto postularía
yo, latinajo o merma, inventaría mecenas para la entraña, dentro de ti leería,
hermano precario, la caja aislada en su blanco por la mira, curta su agua
veloz, apócrifa, cuaje en la frase por segundos, hablando en consecuencia,
qué escurre a cambio, quién anda, si por mula vi cielo, por ras de asfalto
el modo de la sombra cuando se atuvo al mismo bache donde, realismo
obliga, hinqué pie antes de darte de alta, hermano simulado, hoy la barbarie,

Ñ

and the Greco-Roman custom of telling lies
—Gerardo Deniz

So distracting, brutality with its ancient mule, its branch of a dead valley,
coming down the hillside toward you, transitory brother, giving an artful hoof,
jaws restored to their own domain by straw, spitting over the edge
of any type of experience, even the tiniest, grinding away at a light filtered
by the accusing multitude, purge yourself with air, they demand, hunger
before ideas on a stiff road where consciousness cedes its innocuous place
to misery, ill-fated theory, what writing approximates you, solidary brother,
cacophony on the fringes, slash or clean sweep, who decides, no noise at all
without first making sure, sounding hollows, that meekness lingered
here, yearning somewhat, its soft-boned swayback, good judgment
offered as alms, and what I stroked then, cultured brother, on that skin
belonging to another, the Other, if you will, not a brother but a visitor,
lurching heart, was its life as a beginning, first the unmodulated guts,
ringing within that skin regardless, or rasping, damn this savage sun,
as if measuring its retreat in high-pitched minutes along the knife edge
illuminating its metal, rhetorical mule, who'll take away my advantage,
I think as I watch, my fictitious self stroking your back against the grain,
who'll upend the meaning, I brood, it's a querulous brain that makes
formulas, splits in half, a two-headed snake for a straight path, what
hurts is understood, slithers, I'm the one who proposed a mule in a maze,
mumbled Latin or lost profit, invented a patron for heart and soul,
who read within you, precarious brother, eyes on the white space, flog-
    ging its swift, apocryphal
water, curdling the phrase in seconds, speaking accordingly, what
drains out, who goes there, instead of a mule I saw sky, on the asphalt
the shadow's form when it abided by the pothole where, realism

basura multiforme, tieso horizonte de latón, embadurnada lámina bajo

el sitio

de lodo, se engasta en otro símil sublime, polvo casuista, leo, aquella miga

desviada sabiamente por un atajo que es a veces de tiempo, mula de agua,

torcida cuenta, hacia atrás se va retirando una historia, cuánto pan

comido,

aclárame ya si la carencia que he visto es recinto provisorio o costumbre,

¿miento?, revoco mula, otra era de pastizales irá verdeando a la hora

exacta,

titilando, y clientes, niña líbica, niña de marras, mula tuya sea mi cruz,

corren,

que allá promete venderse día por día lo que acumula el monte en años,

trenzándose el rastrojo en libertad, por decirlo de alguna forma, mula,

que mi pascua clandestina busca retoño de espíritu que no cueste o pluma

de qué pájaro entre anillo y anillo, medular, que me salve, mula estática,

de cuánto tumbo por etapas.

compels me to say, I tripped before discharging you, artificial brother,

today's brutality, multifarious garbage, rigid tin horizon, greasy sheet
metal below the mudhole,

is embedded in another sublime simile, casuistic dust, I read, that liquid

wisely shunting off on a shortcut that sometimes is time, watery mule,

twisted bead, behind us a story recedes, what a piece of cake,

tell me now if the poverty I have seen is a makeshift enclosure or a custom,

am I lying?, I revoke my mule, another pastoral age will blossom right on
time, fluttering,

and customers, Lybic daughter, dreary daughter, may your mule be my
cross, come running,

someone's advertising the daily sale of what the hills have accumulated

over years, braiding the stubble freely, to say it one way or another, mule,
my clandestine

veneration searches for tendrils of spirit that will cost me nothing or a feather

from some bird between rings, medullary, that will save me, motionless mule,

from what I wreck in stages.

O

Parecía que mirando las estrellas,
clavada boca arriba en aquel suelo,
estaba a contemplar el curso dellas.
—Garcilaso, Égloga segunda

Qué gorjeas por dentro con el pico clavado, hermano de innumerable
ser, grajo mismo, sustrayendo con la pluma despistada en algún ciclo
de gravedad el truco tras viento de tu forma de alma o gente, cuál
    pausa,
síncopa, pretil con picoteo, labio en tu labio, te atribuyes a la altura
de otro mediodía, místico de sombras desiguales, remero a rastras, renco
tu vuelo por ninguna parte, rayando nidos de golondrina entre un fulgor
de malla y el remanso donde pongo el bulto de mi barrio, ato garra con liga,
roto el ruido, ya resiento quién eres, breve agua por fuero de alguien
que lastima, te quise por ser tú tan ti, vacua laguna del sentido, ahora
ni a la bestia la oyes, su ritmo rapero tan cerca, su rima en colusión con
    el arpa
de ese ángel mediocre que le va creciendo al estuco cada vez que me
    distraigo,
bestia por tanto cielo encima con las cuerdas flojas, tan muerto estornino,
no le nazca otro lienzo virgen, otro vínculo improvisado con la estación
intermedia, sol de azogue que la limite, dos más dos más tres más cinco,
no sumen los doce que voy retirando, hermano de leyes conspicuas,
te absuelvo arena antes de entregarte fragmentos, los duros guijarros
bajo la tácita lluvia, mi bestia en limo, quién litiga con el tambor los
    requisitos
menos modestos de un sonido, ni el tam-tam tiene la sencillez de tu
    vanidad
diferida, siendo eres, lánguida hipótesis de rama en rama hasta tocar piso,

O

Then it seemed to be gazing at the stars,
pinned to the ground, imprisoned on its back,
as if it traced their course over the hours.
—Garcilaso de la Vega, Second Eclogue

What do you warble within, beak to the ground, brother of innumerable

being, you are the raven, your dreamy feather in some gravity loop

abstracting the windy trick, the shape of your soul or person, what

    pause,

syncopated, peck and parapet, lip on lip, do you attribute to another

high noon, mystic of irregular shadows, trailing wing, your feeble

flight to nowhere, scratching out swallows' nests between sunlight

on chain link and the haven where I set down the burden of my

    neighborhood, tether claws with birdlime,

broken babble, I know who you are, brief water decreed by someone

who causes pain, I loved you for being you, meaning's empty pool, now

you don't even hear the beast rapping so close by, its rhymes colluding

    with the harp

of that mediocre angel who blossoms on the stucco whenever I get

    distracted,

beast with so much sky above and loose cords, starling so truly dead,

no place for another blank canvas, improvised link with the middle

season, quicksilver sun that limits it, two plus two plus three plus five,

what if they don't add up to the twelve I take, brother of conspicuous laws,

I absolve you sand before handing over the pieces, hard little pebbles

under tacit rain, my muddy beast, who disputes the least lowly claims

    of a sound

by drumming, not even the steady beat is as simple as your borrowed

vanity, in being you are, languid hypothesis hopping branch to branch

tordo en castigo, bailando de nuevo, aunque se desconozca lo que haya

de ti cuando tañes en mi turno, badajo de más, cuando te apersonas

en la merma de alguna identidad, súbita gente, amodorrado en tus bucles

de célebre cincuentón, moderno repentino, corbata al aire como un
mástil

de tela, dictando oficios en mi sueño de lunes tirano, un ápice de ti
me calcula

en equívocos, noche a destajo voy pidiendo, hermano de mí, no seas
pájaro

que te clavo en la tierra por las puntas, y así porfíes, *avecilla* aprende,

yo te callo.

before touching ground,

chastened robin, dancing once again, although it's unknown what is left

when you ring the bell in my place, one chime too many, take on

a diminished identity, sudden crowd, bleary eyes and the curls

of a fifty-something celebrity, hastily modern, necktie in the air like a cloth

mast, assigning tasks in my despotic Monday dream, an ounce of you
    sums me up

in error, a night of piecework is all I'm asking, brother of mine, don't
    be the bird

whose wings I pin to the ground, and so you struggle, learn, *little bird*,

I'll keep you quiet.

P

Tintineo falso o lámina socavada por un estrépito: de qué hablo, a quién

o cómo, sentimientos son los siguientes, míos bajo piel, tuyos al alcance

de ese dedo que retoba con el eco, sin círculo se añade al repique,

dónde puse la ranura de mi esfera, ande cantando con la aguja en la voz,

no le transfiero el extremo de ninguna pasión, que si es ocaso –vanguardia

concurrida en aquellas sendas del polvo hasta dar con el Chalco increado

de la pura palabra, mi agua y yo, por llamarme– sea provocativa, al menos

histórica, su idea de la fealdad, sea remedo de un desperdicio fastuoso

la chatarra que se acumula en alguna línea de fuego, retoño de fogata,

homérica o cavernosa, prefiérase la gutural cueva a la leyenda, el bisonte

no tiene envergadura en ningún paraíso alternativo, lo sé todo cuando

miento, mi greca reciente es tu hexámetro perdido, ninguna Troya en

estéreo

tendrá la cualidad física del músculo que he visto esbozado en mis

trifulcas,

penumbra moral que restituyo leyendo, miraste esos torsos, amigo de

siglos,

cómo esculpe el miedo su propia playa, mar descendiente, olvido lo

que siento

cuando el espacio, en esquema, dura más allá del risco, entonces engatuso

a mi yo sensible, dulcemente penalizado por la ironía, suéltalo, le exijo,

sé mundo aunque breve, adjetivo espontáneo, ¿ars poetica?, no vaya

seduciendo con su velamen ese cuerpo al concluir, cundiendo el río

en un brazo, primitiva la sal de la comisura o esa máquina de piedra,

ese duelo de dureza, quieres resarcirte, hermano socarrón: una vida

críptica por otra de luces magras, puerto en ángulo donde agua y hábito

suscriben pactos de monotonía, barco distinto sólo si se nombra a

tiempo,

cómo recalamos en este océano construido en caricatura, risco repongo,

P

False clinking or sheet metal corroded by bursts of sound: what am I
    saying, to whom
or how, feelings are the following, mine under skin, yours within reach
of that finger quarreling with echoes, augmenting a peal without a circle,
where did I place the groove of my sphere, shall I walk out singing
    with a needle in my voice,
I assign to it no extremes of passion, and if it's sunset—vanguard
crowding those dusty trails until it gives way to the increate Chalco
of the word itself, my water and me, to name me thus—let its idea of
    ugliness
be provocative, or at least historic, let the junk that accumulates
mimic the remains of a splendid feast, tendrils of a bonfire,
Homeric or cavernous, guttural cave more appealing than legend, bison
inconsequential in any alternative paradise, I know everything when
I'm lying, my just-cut Greek key is your lost hexameter, no Troy in stereo
has the muscular physicality I've seen sketched out in my brawls, moral
penumbra I restore by reading, you watched those torsos, ancient friend,
see how fear carves out its own beach, sloping sea, I forget what I feel
when schematic space lasts beyond the cliff, then I cajole
my sensitive self, sweetly penalized by irony, let it go, I insist,
be the world but be brief, spontaneous adjective, *ars poetica?*, don't let
its specious sails seduce that body in the end, river overflowing
its branch, primitive salt in the corner of an eye or that stone machine,
that enduring duel, you'll try to live it down, sarcastic brother: a cryptic
life in exchange for another of lean lights, angled harbor where water
    and custom
seal their monotonous pacts, a different boat but only if named on time,
how do we reach the shore from this ocean constructed as caricature,
    cliff I recover,

yo no navego en mi naturaleza, duplico ladera por callejón circunscrito,

más poéticamente, hermano meditabundo, la guerra va en tumulto

por la tarde, cuánta hora te embiste, pregonero de la belleza o de los

    métodos

para imitarla, por la mirilla de mí adivino lo que falta para este desierto

en medio, esa franja de vida menos revuelta con sus aspiraciones,

    hermano

de vaivenes, dónde te columbré la última vez, faro ciego o mítica aldea,

quién supo sentir con exactitud, aquí la Historia, allá el refugio

de unas cuantas interpretaciones, *ars* o estrategia, dónde fui dejando

    el molde

de tu mar ceñido, son sentimientos, reclama, pecado por pecado,

¿diste el aguijón o te lo impusieron?

I don't navigate within my nature, I duplicate hillsides inside a circum-
   scribed alley,
more poetically, pensive brother, war runs riot
over the afternoon, how many hours charge at you, heralding beauty
   or the ways
to fake it, through this peephole of mine I can guess what's missing in
   this strip of
desert, that slice of a life scarcely mixing with its aspirations, wavering
brother, where did I last catch sight of you, blind lighthouse or mythic
   village,
who managed to feel precisely, over here History, over there the refuge
of a few interpretations, *ars* or strategy, where did I leave the empty mold
of your narrow-waisted sea, these are feelings, reclaimed, sin by sin,
did you sting yourself or was it imposed upon you?

Q

A la oreja me susurra H.: es el ser del ente, y entiendo yo, monóculo

    tentativo

entre el sol de un absoluto, griego, y las cosas que se miran en la sombra,

hermano iconoclasta, cosas insignificantes, ciertas semillas, una borla de

    pelusa,

estraza esquinera, tal vez un solo zapato, la suela levantisca como lengua

tartamuda en batalla; qué simultáneo resulta filosofar con la incertidumbre,

pregunta: qué es, respuesta: lo que siendo se pregunta por lo que es, y así

prosigue, vadeando en occidente, hermano susceptible, ente que me

    expresa

en ser, todo reside en el vocablo, insiste H., aporía o entelequia, elija la

    señora

al calce, la lista de atributos no cambia según el caso, camino al ente se llega

filosofando al mismo recodo, pregunta en pos de su cola ¿será víbora

    enrollada

en su propia comedia de víbora?, de ahí la oscuridad queda a campo

    traviesa,

por la trinchera del pasto, por el montículo de tierra, agua que da lo mismo,

señora o doncella quisquillosa, escoja, ponga las cuatro zonas de su alma

–iguales para todos, me advierte H.– en el cuenco quieto del ente,

    póngalas

de mañana, bajo el sol de soles, se alumbre la aporía con su entelequia,

ni yo retrocedo con tanta luz enajenada por su definición, esencia o

    carbunclo

aquello que brilla íntimamente en el tiradero, a su manera combustible, arde

con un guiño de razón, señora ausente, ¿por la ventana interpósita me

    percibe?

o estoy, sicomoro aparte, por decir, manantial sin plata cuando el ente

    se colma

Q

H. whispers in my ear: it is the being of entities, and I understand,
    tentative monocle
between the glare of an absolute, Greek, and the things that are seen
    in shadow,
iconoclastic brother, worthless things, some seeds, a ball of lint,
rags on the corner, perhaps a single shoe, sole like a stuttering
tongue in battle; how simultaneous, to philosophize with uncertainty,
question: what is it, answer: it is what, in being, asks what it is, and so
it goes, wading into the west, sensitive brother, entity who expresses
    me in being,
it all depends on the choice of words, insists H., aporia or entelechy,
    let the lady choose,
the list of attributes doesn't change according to the case, the road
to entity ends in the same philosophical cul-de-sac, a question chasing
    its tail, is it a snake
coiled into its own parody of a snake?, from there the darkness rests
    cross country,
in the grassy trench, on the mound of earth, it's water all the same,
mature lady or finical maiden, choose, set down the four zones of your soul
—the same for everyone, H. advises me—within entity's quiet hollow,
    set them down
in daylight, under the sun of suns, aporia illuminated with its entelechy,
I can't even retreat before so much light alienated by its definition,
    essence or diamond
shining intimately, combustibly, atop the garbage heap, burning with
a knowing wink, abstracted lady, do you see me through the window
    that divides us?
or am I, apart from the sycamore, so to speak, a silverless spring when
    entity floods with mud,

de lodo, en la figura que pasa, atada a la lógica, no sea tanta personalidad

un riesgo, señala H., atiborre al ser, lo desprenda de sus ídolos más útiles,

con saña de vericueto, ahueque la hipótesis, jalando mi sicomoro,

    piedad,

hacia un árbol de menos, cuánta haya en el trueque por el borde liviano,

voy reticente de mí, raíz entablada en ángulo contra la superficie, cuánto

me anima el garabato, señora de la cueva, me retiene en su circo complejo,

por ente en su carpa me entrometo, que nada cuesta la sintaxis en esta

    curva

aguda, oliendo a payaso en la pista, huyo, señora, esto se acabó:

sólo cupo el ser que quiso.

in the passing figure, tied to logic, so much personality shouldn't be

a risk, H. notes, cramming into being, peeling away from its most useful

idols, spiteful shortcut, hollowing out the hypothesis, dragging my

    sycamore, mercy,

toward a lesser tree, how many beeches in exchange for the light edge,

reluctant I go, root angled against the surface, see how the

scribble animates me, lady of the cave, holds me in its complex circus,

disguised as an entity I squeeze into the tent, syntax costs me nothing

    on this sharp

curve, smelling like clowns on a racetrack, I'm leaving, lady, it's all over:

only the being who tried was able to fit.

R

para escurrirse por la tez del mundo
hacia los ojos de los nadadores
—Héctor Viel Temperley

Son espigones a tu alcance, hábil conjeturo, o modestas rutas de cloro
para una finita brazada, hermano vagabundo, que ya ni salpica el agua
referente, ni retiene brisa el escuadrón de avionetas cuando repinta
en su extremo la imagen de este cielo, y yo, óyeme, ya ni tengo hora
para reponer el arco de arena o, rizando el rizo, la mitra alusiva entre rayos
y deslaves, ni cordel, exagerando, para el descenso, niña en trenza, ni
   manual
de vituperios, rostro de calle, día de días; son casi 45 las veces entonces
en que te admiro, a espaldas, hermano agorero, ¿eres o no eres?,
   siquiera desata
el chisme, un siglo XX de tarde, siquiera da ejemplos, estuvo
no la infancia, sino la silueta que divide un año en otro, el ego de ti,
adivino, casi la escafandra que te endiosa en otra agua fluctuante,
casi la alegoría que te explica antes de rotular el aviso: aquí se prescinde
de andamio, psicología en chusma, se renta a conciencia, se divulga charco
en traspatio, fácil traspié a orillas de tu sitio, tu finta de azul, tu lustre
en balde al amanecer como una costumbre que ya no se retoma, hermano
   espía,
niña tenue, vayan temiendo a los adversarios hoy, la horda
entre barda y barda, no declame ese mar de manos una consigna
que revuelva vidrio con púa, sangre con palo y hacha, no te esfumes
niña por arte de magia en mi episodio 45, sagradamente mitigo
en tu causa las rachas de letargo con una pizca de vicio, memoria de ti
en mi cristal de autorretratos, cómo esgrimo la máscara entre personaje
y gente, fútil año de utilería con la alberca a mitad de un mes incoloro

R

To drain through the face of the world
towards the eyes of the swimmers
—Héctor Viel Temperley (trans. Stuart Krimko)

Jetties are within your reach, my clever surmise, or modest trails of chlorine
for the swimmer's finite crawl, vagabond brother, now that this water
won't splash, nor the aerial squadron hold the breeze
when it writes its message on this sky, and hear me, I don't have time
to replace the arc of sand or, looping the loop, the allusive crown
between rays and rockfalls, nor a cord, to exaggerate, for my descent,
    braided daughter, nor a manual
of insults, street face, day of days; thus have I contemplated you
almost 45 times, behind your back, doomsday brother, do you or do
    you not exist?, at least stir up
the gossip, a 20th-century afternoon, give examples, what we had was
not childhood, only a silhouette between years, ego of yours,
I guess, almost the wetsuit that deifies you in another fluctuating
water, almost the allegory that explains you before lettering the sign:
Caution No Scaffolding Here, no trailer-park psychology, this space
    thoroughly for rent, seller discloses a puddle
in the yard, easy stumble on the fringes of your site, blue feint, luster
at daybreak, pointless as a long-abandoned local custom, spy brother,
shy daughter, who's afraid of an adversary today, the horde
inside the castle walls, don't let the sea of hands intone a rallying cry,
glass with barbed wire, blood with cudgel and ax, daughter don't
disappear as if by magic in my 45th chapter, sacredly on your behalf
I leaven these spells of lethargy with a pinch of vice, memory of you
in my mirror of self-portraits, see how I wield the mask between character
and person, useless year of props, swimming pool in a colorless month,

en su foto de costa pobre, de palapa en ruina, no se mira claro, háblame

hermano, tu yate en binocular algo revela de los ideales, su firme

tendencia individual que no caduca, supongo, en esta tromba,

sucedánea de alguna suerte, tormenta de lares casi por rutina,

la mía la leo: veinte veces entraré conmigo en la misma náutica trillada,

veinte más haré de río por la cintura de esa playa al sesgo y tuya

será la turbulencia cuando tiemble aquel bimotor en la casilla

de mi viento, luego yo nadaré de cinco en cinco.

blurred photo of an impoverished coast, a ruined palapa, talk to me

brother, your distant yacht reveals something about ideals, their firm

individual tendency, not lapsing, I suppose, in this downpour,

a substitute for luck, an almost habitual storm of superstition,

I read my fortune: twenty times I will sail with myself on the same stale sea,

twenty more I will make me a river on the waist of that sloping beach,

and yours will be the turbulence when the twinjet shakes

in the chamber of my wind, then I will swim by fives.

S

¿Y la tibia latitud con la basura por delante? ¿el crimen, melodrama o saga?
¿la sabiduría resuelta por la simpleza de una anécdota? ¿la inculta reseña
de un paisaje disminuido por su avidez?, hermano sutil, ¿has notado
cuánto presentimiento se introduce en las múltiples versiones del mundo?,
esta provincia de envergadura o tu aldea retraída como un sabueso tímido
que no se atreve a caerle encima a su presa, de qué sirve mencionarlas
si no representan un caso, yo vivo aquí, tú allá eres fragmento de donde
yo recorto identidades, lugar o imagen, por ejemplo, la falsa alhambra
de tu memoria, la leída, ese manantial recurrente, apócrifo, los animales
en procesión por la piedra rosa, la grieta embestida por el plomo de un clavo
a distancia, qué cuelga, niña rota, señora en pináculo, qué diestra condena
sin precisar el hoyo y en qué muro, quién enumera sustantivos, una vez
por arrogancia, otra por melancolía, y figurándose un horizonte con tintes
mediterráneos, flancos toscanos a mitad de un hito defeño, se toca la frente
con el dedo de su nostalgia sublime, todo visto por entresijos, por astucia,
el declive abrupto, el desenlace ingenioso del asfalto, miren, clama, ¡Piazza!,
combinando el resuello con un acento ladino, tanto hermano listo, mi niña
en oscuro, este país cede su fórmula de enigmas a quien la pague,
esos misterios no cuestan o se rehacen a la primera mengua del sentido,
luz, tras la ambarina huella, se escapa, tras la hierba de un baldío, pasa
como ayer, en otro tiempo, hermano, ya presente, disuelto en los hechos,
qué colinda al tanteo con esta raya en medio de la avenida, esta casa
    modesta
en la colonia, esta cortina en movimiento con un pliegue a ras del aire
donde ocurre una fracción de siglo, sin ceremonia, qué dispara aconte-
    cimientos
como si los hubiera diseñado una mente incapaz de rumiar con las manos,
qué pared en tirol se resiste a la mustia reminiscencia de la suavidad
cuando voy contigo, hermano, procurando cierta fe en la fe, el territorio

S

And the warm latitude brimming with garbage? crime, melodrama, or

saga? wisdom resolved by the simplest anecdote? uncouth outline

of a landscape lessened by its greed?, subtle brother, have you noticed

how much premonition creeps into the multiple versions of the world?,

this province of high consequence or your village drawn back like a

hound too timid to fall upon its prey, why bring these things up if they

don't represent a case, I live here, you are a fragment of where

I cut out identities, place or image, for example, the false alhambra

of your memory, as it is read, apocryphal, recurrent spring, animals

in procession over the pink stone, crack assailed by a distant nail,

what is hung, broken daughter, lady on a pinnacle, what hand condemns

without specifying the hole or wall, who enumerates nouns, once

for arrogance, twice for melancholy, picturing a Mediterranean

horizon, Tuscan hills in Mexico City, touches his forehead

with the finger of his sublime nostalgia, seeing as if spying, in cunning,

abrupt slope, asphalt's ingenious finale, look, he calls, *Piazza!*,

combining his gasps with a wily giggle, such a smart brother, my daughter

in the dark, this country offers up its formula of enigmas for a price,

the mysteries cost nothing or are rebuilt when meaning starts to wane,

light, behind the amber residue, escapes, behind the wasteland,

happens just like yesterday, in another time, brother, premonition

    dissolved

into fact, what roughly abuts this line in the center of the avenue, this

    modest house

in the suburbs, this curtain in motion, its folds flush with the air

where the fraction of a century occurs, unceremonious, what shoots

    out events

as if designed by a mind incapable of ruminating with its hands,

what stuccoed wall resists sullen memories of softness

lleno de gente, alguien a ratos intrigado por esa porción de biografía
prometida, en otro sitio su vida iba a imitar el orden de su propio relato:
*aquí nací en la comarca, líbrela el divino de cualquier nombre, a palos eché
a los traidores, a palos maté a los viejos y a los enemigos,* un auténtico
   héroe
de este mundo que me representa pero no conozco, salvo por su moral
ambigua a veces, cuando oigo aquel rumor de que algunas tradiciones
de la bondad incluyen el escarmiento por contradecirlas con un acto
no aludido de misericordia, niña nítida: aquí sucede únicamente lo que sucede.

when I go with you, brother, procuring a kind of faith in faith, territory
teeming with people, someone intrigued by that promised bit
of biography, where his life would follow its own narration:
I was born here in this region, may God save it from being named, with
  this cudgel
I cast out traitors, with this cudgel I killed old men and my enemies, an
  authentic hero of this world
that represents but is unknown to me, except by its sometimes
ambiguous morality, when I hear the rumor that certain traditions
of kindness include punishment contradicted by an unacknowledged
act of mercy, clear-cut daughter: here only what happens happens.

T

Que estuvo en Utopía, presume, periódico bajo el brazo, mi hermano

viajero, horas de espera, recalca, la mente en blanco, la duda inscrita

como método, dos islas, dos ciudades, repetido el pasmo, dos atalayas

entre puerta y puerta, norte invadido por la fila de anhelantes, sur
    desviado

hacia una hondonada, agua en brotes por cada brecha; que estuvo en
    secreto,

disimulando el tedio: tanto lema espiritual entre pórticos, peristilos, el
    retiro

de los claustros, no condujo más que a sustitutos, hermano caviloso,
    pulcras

metafísicas donde nunca contaría el cerebro que las sostuvo, y tú y yo

y ellos, hartos del giro impecable, la horma del universo en la cabeza

igual a la dimensión de los ritos empleados para convocarla, no seríamos

ni siquiera uno, ni siquiera tú, Utopía o isla en luna creciente, mutilando

la llanura exquisita cuando recitabas, guiño en vez de gesto, hermano
    refinado,

lo indemostrable: la república de seres perfectos, pensados, primero,
    descritos,

en seguida, cuando iban por la calle, humanamente sencillos, sin asomo

entre ceja y ceja, rala paradoja, de algún dilema ético, aunque malos hoy,

leyendo entre líneas al prójimo, sabiéndolo todo, cómo miente cuando
    afirma

la verdad; barroca Utopía la que van imaginando, barroca isla aunque
    tenue

tan pronto recurre a las trampas de una claridad que nadie agradece,

para qué entender, oscuro el oficio de la bondad, niña tente en pie,
    amaga

Utopía su propio escondite, has visto cuando llegan los seres perfectos

T

He's come from Utopia, gloating, newspaper tucked under his arm,
   my brother
the traveler, hours spent waiting, he insists, mind a blank, doubt inscribed
as a method, two islands, two cities, repeated shock, two watchtowers
between the entrances, north invaded by the line of supplicants,
   south diverted
into a gully, water gushing through every gap; he was there in secret,
hiding his boredom: so many spiritual maxims between porticos,
   peristyles, the calm
of cloisters, leading to nothing more than substitutes, neurotic brother, tidy
metaphysics in which the brain that sustained them never mattered,
   and you and I
and them, fed up with the impeccable turning, the form of the universe
   in our heads
equal in dimension to the rites used to summon it, there we would be
not even me, not even you, Utopia or island below a waxing moon,
   mutilating
the exquisite plain while you recited, with a wink instead of a wave,
   refined brother,
the indemonstrable: a republic of perfect beings, imagined first, described
next, as they made their way down the street, humanly simple, no hint
between their brows, scanty paradox, of any ethical quandary, though
   they are evil today,
reading each other between the lines, knowing it all, how one lies
   while insisting on
the truth; it's a baroque Utopia they imagine, baroque island that
   nonetheless weakens
when resorting to the traps of a clarity that no one is thankful for,
why try to understand, kindness is a dark trade, daughter get up,

a este lodazal de lluvia, su elocuencia, limo en la boca, la has notado,

cuánto articulan las palabras destino, grandeza, valentía, que labrando

futuro se gastará mejor cualquier trunca conjetura del mundo, lo que sea

en esencia, repítelo, maestro o mimo, Utopía tuvo su centro pertinaz

en un revuelo de teorías, su íntima agua en borrador por los costados,

corriendo el tiempo con esa aptitud para prolongarse más allá

de las predicciones, mañana serás bueno, hermano inconstante,

en Utopía no hay lugar para los ilusos, nadie se lo explica, tras cabaña,

tras choza que linda con la cueva, primavera en principio lasciva

con sus injertos, su flor multitudinaria, su río adulterado por las luces,

calla hermano, qué premura para opinar civilizadamente, hoy

no es lo que parece, prensa transcribe toda semejanza con la realidad,

he visto que ayer siempre ocurre al día siguiente, hermano perogrullo,

tinta no soporta tu letanía de virtudes en retroceso hasta un origen

    inmaculado,

donde mundo es un jueves, augura, triple dado, y si se dispersa el azul

que empuñas como si fuera posible arrebatarlo, una atmósfera menos

liviana, áspera al tacto, intervendría con su brote provisional quizá

de cielo vagamente más viejo.

Utopia lies hidden, have you seen the perfect beings come

to this rainy slough, their eloquence, muddy mouthed, have you noticed,

how they articulate the words destiny, grandeur, valor, by forging

a future they'll end up wasting some maimed conjecture of the world,

in essence, repeat it, maestro or mime, Utopia found its pertinacious center

in a whirl of theory, its intimate water a marginal note,

time running with that ability to prolong itself beyond

all predictions, tomorrow you'll be good, inconstant brother, Utopia

has no place for dreamers, no one explains why, behind the shack,

behind the hut bordering on the cave, a springtime lecherous in principle

with its grafted trunks, its manifold flower, its river adulterated by lights,

keep quiet brother, what's your rush to venture a civilized opinion, today

is not what it seems, the press transcribes every likeness to reality,

yesterday always takes place tomorrow, platitudinous brother,

ink will not bear your litany of virtues retreating into its immaculate origins,

where world is a Thursday, foretelling, triple dice, and if the blue

you clutch as if you could pull it down should disperse, a less light

atmosphere, rough to the touch, would perhaps intervene with its

    provisional gush

of an indistinctly older sky.

U

Me elucida cara en discordia, diablo babeando hasta en la leche, afuera

la lluvia, adentro la sardónica evidencia de las paradojas, pan duro, mojigata

la señora me cuenta, yo mirando su escote hundido en la grasa del cuello,

pan suave entre los dientes, pica de nuevo, hocico, dos o tres epigramas,

muñón de concha, como si nada una ventisca que remeda en los manteles

la sutileza de la gasa, me describe, paloma y polvo, lo *genuinamente*

    mexicano,

y oigo pensando, ese apelativo que se me pega con un laberinto adicional

en la oreja, solariego entre mis bastidores, ese rito de cascos y coronas,

será la nación, mi señora de tiza, de borla, de esquila, lo será esa resolana

entre tabiques, esa racha de mala política, ese difuso grafiti de alguna idea

de país camino a la tiesura de una pancarta, *¿genuinamente mexicano?,*

    señora

lírica, por mi parque de arboledas divulga una rata la misma historia,

    allende

el monte, ¿hortelano en un jubileo de arroyos o égloga distraída por el

    saqueo

de sus habitantes?, la pregunta afirma su contrario, he visto, señora

    coqueta,

cómo una estructura, discursiva en su descenso, se inmiscuye en mi

    colonia

y acaba haciendo patria, bocacalle, vecindario, melodía breve, rancio

    musgo,

cómo la rata de hoy, deambulando entre troncos antes de evolucionar

hacia la ardilla, se extiende hasta mañana, escarba cuánta leyenda diminuta

en su pesquisa, señora de estopa, y resuelve: sobra el futuro, ¡tanto y luego

tanto!, por quién toca, a la puerta, y qué puerta, de aldabones, qué inmensa

puerta la que se abre hacia fuera, mundo por fin, mexicanamente,

aunque yo no genuina, amortiguo la caída, voy, ya voy, anda, tiéntame,

U

Poised to enlighten me is the dissonant face, devil slobbering even in
    the milk, outside
the rain, within the sardonic evidence of paradox, stale bread, priggish
lady who tells me, as I gaze at the cleavage submerged in her fatty neck,
soft bread between her teeth, another sliver, snout, two or three epigrams,
stumpy sweet roll, just like that a gust on the tablecloths mimicking
the delicacy of chiffon, she describes to me, dove and dust, *the genuine*
    Mexican,
and I hear her, thinking: that sobriquet sticking to me like another labyrinth
in my ear, ancestral seat waiting in my wings, rite of crests and crowns,
is that the nation, my lady of chalk, of tassels, shards, is it that swelter
of thin walls, spell of bad politics, diffuse graffiti of an idea
of a country on its way to becoming as rigid as a placard, *the genuine*
    Mexican?, lyric
lady, within my wooded park a rat divulges the same story, over the
    mountain,
orchard keeper in a jubilee of streams or eclogue distracted by the
    massacre
of its inhabitants?, the question affirms its opposite, I've seen, coy lady,
the way that a structure, discursive in its descent, encroaches on my
    suburban turf
and ends up making a fatherland, side street, neighborhood, brief
    melody, musty moss,
the way that today's rat, sauntering among tree trunks before evolving
into a squirrel, extends until tomorrow, digs up each miniscule legend in its
investigations, my lady of burlap, and resolves: there's too much future!,
knock knock, who's there, what a door, what a big brass knocker,
immense door opening outwards, the world at last, how very Mexican,
although I'm not genuine, I cushion the fall, I'm really going, tempt me,

diablo de marras, dime qué mitad de mí corresponde a este paraje nacional,

pues vivo de su cauda y mi resquemor en la sortija de su lumbre se parece

a un tributo que le rinde un instante geométrico al resto de una sombra,

padre o madre, me comentan que hay fronteras internas y externas,

un destino de la línea, buena, mala, cuánto daría por saberlo, adoquín

bajo el ansia, ¿licenciado o poeta?, declárese que hay híbridas multitudes

que conciben su espíritu variopinto de modo unitario, siempre cuchicheando

por la estrofa y más vivo que nunca, afirman zarpa en mano,

ésos que lo regatean.

dreary devil, say which half of me corresponds to this expanse of nation,

as I live in its train and my resentment under its diamond light seems like

a tribute lending a geometric instant to the remnants of a shadow,

father or mother, telling me there are borders internal and external,

fate along the line, good, bad, I wish I knew, cobblestone

beneath the anguish, scholar or poet?, there are hybrid multitudes

who conceive of their multifarious spirit in unison, always whispering

with every stanza and alive as ever, clamoring claw in hand,

those hagglers.

V

Es la V de vado, de vagancia, de venganza, de varada, de vahído, de valla,

de vente, de vino, de va, de nuevo: mi instinto, por el amor de los otros,

mi calle en el mundo, por las manos entreveradas con la noción de un

   tiempo

y el peso de una pena, ¿verdad tangible?, me burlo, veinte días avisté

la línea tenue entre mi casa y la región ajena, grandilocuente, veinte días

de vuelta me dije, esto hiede a ganga, melodrama y tragedia en un solo

vuelco de ruedas, hermano veloz, cuéntame tu vida, es demasiado tarde,

ya comienza el episodio mudo, recalcas, leyendo hasta que termine,

en ese mullido sillón se retrae cualquier personaje, el quién de ayer,

pegado a la tele, canal por canal, sujeto a un actor de reparto, bigote

postizo, qué peluca sin rango luminoso, qué beso en los labios de un

   espejo,

qué guiño entre neón y cigarro, humo manso por la corriente, mi pensativo,

mi taimado, asesina mujeres en un baldío, mi amigo, hermano, mira

decapitaciones en videos clandestinos, de aquí me voy, de aquí paso

a la página, al quién de ahora, lince perspicaz, le repito a sus letras,

gato obligatorio y lúcido, garra en ristre, lemur o mantra, según desee

bienestar el alma, recítale como si estuviera sola: *tanta mente que el*

   cuerpo

nimio es apenas teatro de pesquisa moral, alma la panza de un dios

   de todos,

la adulo, tripa sin tesituras, le propongo, y a cada actitud un gruñido,

voy, vengo de cínica por la carne ahíta, romántico responso, voy

de hambre, de mística vengo, de noche por el cuarto, escala al cielo,

mi peldaño tendrá el mármol de otra nieve, la posterior, cuánto

cuesta esculpir suficientes arcaísmos para inquietar al ejecutante

moderno, fortalezas luidas por la bruma, basta de mofas, pido pausa,

por buscar lo más simple di contigo, siendo un silencio, ya no va.

V

V is for vessel, for vassal, for vengeance, for vast, is for vertigo, verge,

is for veer, is for venture, for voyage, de novo: my instinct, my love for others,

my place in the world, my hands clasping a vague sense of time

and the weight of sorrow, a tangible truth?, I'm only joking, twenty

    days I divined the fine line

joining my house to everything outside, grandiloquent, twenty days

back I muttered, this stinks like a bargain, melodrama and tragedy in a

turn of the wheel, vanishing brother, how have you lived, too late,

it's time for the silent film, you insist, reading until the final credits,

any character would get swallowed up in that easy chair, any has-been,

glued to the TV, changing channels, subject to a character actor, paste-on

mustache, lusterless toupee, kiss-kiss on the mirrored lips, wink-wink with

the neon and cigar, slow smoke on the water, my pensive one, my sly one,

chopping up women on a lonely hill, my friend, my brother, watching

beheadings on blurry videotape, here's where I veer away, revert to the

page, the here and now, observant lynx, I join my voice to the letters,

omnipresent and clearsighted cat, paw at the ready, lemur or mantra,

    however the soul

desires its peace, tell its tale as if all alone: *so much mind that the body*

is barely a trivial theater for moral investigations, soul the belly of a

    universal god,

I adore it, gut untouched by nuance, I propose it, and a grunt for every

    change of stance,

I voyage, I veer like a cynic into sated flesh, romantic requiem, I voyage

into hunger, veer into mysticism, the room at night, ladder to heaven,

my step as alabaster as a different snow, a future snow, how much

will it cost to sculpt sufficient archaisms to trouble the modern

performer, bulwarks brushed by mist, joking aside, I pray you, pause,

seeking the simplest solution I saw you, a silence, once removed.

W

Hay algo indecente en la esencia misma de la poesía

—Czeslaw Milosz

Y si cambio de ritmo, can-can diezmado por la canícula de un incendio
tan simbólico que apesta a viejo, a ropa de muerto, a miedo en trance
por su invasora mañana, pandilla en fresco, punta de lanza, lánguidamente
lastrando con alguna ley cotidiana, tácita, la mescolanza de rasgos entre agua
y piel, tobillo, codo, pantorrilla, y hacia abajo los perros de un infierno culto
que arrebatan retazos: mía la muñeca, el muslo, ah, lumbre de todos,
ladrido de diez a doce, mordiendo su propia sombra quisiera remedar
las fuentes de un solo odio legendario, hermano y prójimo, mi primer día
estuvo en ascuas por canjear la luz de donde vino cuando sonaba a festín
de niños pasajeros en el recreo, retumbando su ciega, su azul medida
entre columpio y pico, cavando ojo en su acero, mirándome, ese animal
no lo hice yo, di luz por piernas, tentativamente, bailando en este pasillo
de casa en casa, no lo hice, mis mentiras tuvieron tiempo de dilatarse,
inventaron su propia muralla, su país vecino, su moneda bastarda,
hasta una nieve distinta, fragmentada, blanca sólo en las esquinas,
su país de nadie, ayer casi pierdo el camino, corrígeme si no, hermano,
cuántos pasos, vueltas, taconeos, can-can de chispa y llama, voy por mi casa
como si fuera la tuya, me has tocado con la música metida en un rincón
de la voz, tras de mí, así va, no una melodía, la vida de hoy, martes,
cuando suena halla consuelo en las porciones más pequeñas del espacio
otorgado, bajo mesa, bajo silla, ahí extiende otro polvo, un ruido más astuto,
perro absuelto, perro de agua santa, colmillo en la raja de sol, aquí tanto
vi que si cambio me pongo de más: otra piedra añadida a la gente.

W

In the very essence of poetry there is something indecent
—Czeslaw Milosz (trans. Czeslaw Milosz & Lillian Vallee)

And what if I change the rhythm, can-can decimated by a dog-days blaze
so symbolic it smells old, like a dead man's clothes, fear entranced
by its invading morning, gang of thugs freshly created, spear point, languidly
ballasting with a tacit workaday law, hodgepodged features of water
and skin, ankle, elbow, calf, and down below the dogs of a cultured hell
pulling off pieces: mine the wrist, the thigh, ah, light from all of them,
barking from ten to twelve, biting their own shadows they try to mimic
the origins of a single legendary hatred, brother and other, my first day
was itching to swap the light it came from when it sounded like a parade
of happy children at recess, roaring its blind, blue measure between
swing and summit, gouging an eye on steel, watching me, I didn't make
that animal, I gave light not legs, tentative, dancing the distance
from house to house, I didn't do it, my lies had time enough to expand,
invented their own great wall, neighboring nation, bastard currency,
even a different snow, fragmented, barely white, their own no man's land,
yesterday I almost lost my way, correct me if I'm wrong, brother,
how many steps, turns, heel taps, can-can flaring, I pace my house
as if it were yours, you have touched me with the music in a corner of
your voice, behind me it goes, not a melody, today's life, Tuesday's,
rings and is consoled by the smallest conceded space,
under tables, under chairs, a different dust, a smarter sound,
absolved dog, holy-water dog, tooth in a slice of sun, I saw so much here if I
change I'll be one too many: one more stone on the pile of people.

X

De la noche a la mañana voy
sacando lengua a las más mudas equis.

—César Vallejo

Río a rebato, he puesto hueso de ala entre la cresta y la espuma,
levanto el resto, debajo pulo, corto, rebano, ¿hay testigos?, ira aparte,
limo el tajo, mondo la escara, recaudo entre costra y mata seca la airada
pluma, el moribundo remero, ¿qué siento?, élitro o córnea, da lo mismo
cuando el índice desmiente al pulgar, desviando elijo la grada más alta,
el tableteo adentro simula un aire mínimo, vuela tierra por su lado franco,
el tirón de músculo es de viento y piel, va tu cara de por medio, señas,
hermano, más señas, no vaya a resultar simbolista este paisaje,
trepo monte, arisca mi fortuna, si hubiera la ruina al menos
de un monumento, pero este trayecto, tuyo hasta la tarde, luce
opaco a falta de ingenio, ¿eres tú?, pobre mito, mi alambique se busca
rebelde algún artífice, habrá oficio más provechoso, copista, sastre,
vendedor, por las ramas me restrinjo, distraigo octubre, claridades
para ganarme al bicho de la usura, libarlo, río de canto rombo, si supiera
que lo de hoy es historia mañana afinaría el gesto, señas, mi niña díscola,
que nace tímida la razón, que nace mutua la culpa, ojos grandes, entrecejo
lunático, boca tirando hacia la risa, pido constancia, sea mercurial
la más bella, prófuga aunque absoluta en su instante, labor de los afectos,
quererte aquí, por obediencia, refugiarme allá, en remilgo de bodegones,
cuando se pierde el ímpetu, la bondad incierta de ir agradeciendo,
derrochando río, agua lisa a veces tan última, si se regara a cántaros
como nunca ocurre devolvería mi obsequio: esa persona, tildada
de mí en la orilla, que me ve siempre pasar.

X

From night to morning I am sticking
out my tongue at the mutest X's.
—César Vallejo (trans. Rebecca Seiferle)

River, ring out the alarm, I place the wing bone between crest and foam,
I lift the rest, underneath I polish, cut, slice, are there witnesses?, setting
    rage aside,
I smooth the gash, swab the sore, from crust and brush I pluck the furious
feather, the dying wing, what do I feel?, elytron or cornea, it's all the same
when the index finger calls the thumb a liar, I change course, head higher,
the rattle within simulates a minimal air, earth flies over its open side,
muscle pulled by wind and skin, your face before me, signs,
brother, more signs, don't let this landscape turn out to be symbolist,
I climb the hill, my fortune fierce, if only there were at least the ruins
of a monument, but this pathway, yours until the afternoon, has lost its
shine for want of wit, is that you?, poor myth, my alembic searches,
rebellious, for an inventor, a more rewarding line of work, scrivener, tailor,
salesman, in the branches I restrain myself, distract October, clarities
to win over the pest of usury, sip it slowly, round-shouldered river, if I knew
today's news is tomorrow's history I'd refine the gesture, signs, disobedient
daughter, reason is born timid, guilt is born mutual, big eyes, lunatic
brow, mouth twisting in laughter, I ask for certainty, the beautiful
may be mercurial, fugitive but absolute, a work of affection,
loving you here, out of obedience, seeking shelter there, in a fretful still life,
having lost momentum, the dubious kindness of perpetually giving thanks,
letting the river spill, glassy water at times so final, if it came pouring down
like it never does, it would return my offering: that person, branded
with my name, on the bank, always watching me walk by.

Y

y el agua harapienta de los pies secos
—Federico García Lorca

Óyelo, hermano, cómo se madreperla oblicuando su filón de granito
en las zonas bajas, cómo se corusca, se arrisca, se lastima, va de lengua
en idiomatismo retumbando por el surco con su forma de roca
en rumbo, cómo se desempieza al organizar otro principio, cantarino
en loma ajena, mudando ovejas por tramo de calles, cuánto bala,
hermano de nítidas causas, oye y defínelo en consecuencia, ¿amaga
el orto o es mera luz de nuevo en el matadero?, agua a contrapelo,
hocico a tiempo para el despilfarro, los ríos de la sangre no corren así,
según mi libro de ciencia, ah, realista, yo desplume por paja a mi gallo
trashumante y luego, náyade al fin, gane corriente en calidad de ofrenda,
quizás engañe pero conmisero, tanto sol por metáfora, sensible sol,
no caduca con los hechos, aunque duela el renco tedio de su belleza
a mediodía, cuando toco el vidrio empalmado con la figura más cercana,
y me digo, se siente la fría, blanca, muda merma de la materia,
va siendo hora, niña severa, de entrometer la pasión donde sólo
raya el día, lo aconsejan amigos, tregua del cálculo, que nadie
se engaste en aquel nicho de los sentidos, cancelando mi pretexto
para un ambiguo conocimiento de cualquier barbarie, no vaya a faltar
cuerda para enredar mi escepticismo con fórmulas socarronas, divísame,
hermano, hay hados silvestres en esta banqueta o la moraleja es otra:
por la razón se comparte un mínimo indicio de odio;
yo peco por ti, el prójimo lo sabe.

Y

and the water, dressed in rags, but with dry feet
—Federico García Lorca (trans. Greg Simon & Steven F. White)

Listen, brother, how it mother-of-pearls slanting its granite vein into
the low zones, coruscates, leaps the crags, suffers wounds, spouts
idioms, roars through the furrow in the shape of a rock on course,
how it unbegins another beginning, sings out on a hill belonging
to another, herding sheep through the street, so much bleating,
brother of clear-cut causes, listen and then define it, impending
sunrise or just a light switched on in the slaughterhouse?, water against
     the grain,
prodigal muzzle at the ready, rivers of blood don't flow that way, or so says
my science book, such a realist, if I witlessly pluck my transhumant
rooster and then, a naiad in the end, receive the current as an offering,
I may mislead but I do commiserate, so much metaphorical, sensitive sun
never expires with the facts, though at noon the hamstrung boredom of its
beauty hurts, when I touch the window joined to the nearest figure,
and tell myself, you can feel the cold, white, silent diminishment of matter,
it's high time, severe daughter, to let passion intrude where only
the day breaks, friends advise it, cease calculating, no one
deserves to be embedded in that niche of sense, annulling my pretext
for an ambiguous understanding of brutality, don't forget the
rope to entangle my skepticism with cunning formulas, attend me,
brother, this sidewalk breeds wild fates or else the moral changes:
through reason the slightest trace of hatred is shared;
I sin for you, the others know this.

Z

Aquélla fue la hora más demente
—Ungaretti

Que te apartes un poco y no me quites el sol, te pido, cínico de tinaja,
que vayas rematando a cuanto pájaro vacuo de mí se asome
entre la mañana y la noche, pues no tengo más bufón que darte,
y ya me cacarea otra criatura, ya me susurra otro ídolo menos falso:
tanta agua quebrada, hermano irresuelto, niña del alba, parece
la trampa de un espejo, otro brillo entre la moneda y la mortaja,
pero eres pulga de dioses, me dice, no luz propia, no bestia congénita,
y al hilo de mar negro en tu cubo, lo he visto extinguirse, he tocado
a la interpósita, primitiva, figura de un cuerpo, señora indolente,
rascando por debajo el mundo tiene sus razones, cuánto pululan,
por intriga conceden misterio: una edad de oro, no cuaja eso, acoge
al perro ¿Diógenes? ¿o el disfraz, mueca y guiño, de un atildado
   publicista?,
a ratos mi bípedo implume divulga populismo, ácido amor
por nosotros, óyelo, cómo lo anuncia, tarima de por medio,
sus *antes* supremos, la pureza de otro régimen, cuánto tunde
con su paño de estameña, su alforja hueca, su pergamino en balde,
aunque hubo reverbero de centavos, pienso en desagravio, aplauso,
de púlpito en púlpito, mi pregonero de la lumbre misma, ritual y roja,
pudo cobrarle al tiempo lo que le sobra, mi adivina, herraje o calle,
alguna verdad que desconozco, por aquí, repito, en este laberinto
de provincia, donde mi hermano trenza, niña de comarca, su humo
oportunista con el solo aspaviento: ¡una ocurrencia!, y urde finales
por convención, señora, leyendo, su verosímil cuño en el aire
quizá transmute valores, purgue ideas con un ejemplo, al menos
lúcidamente las postergue, ¿para quién?,

Z

That was the most demented hour
—Ungaretti (trans. Diego Bastanutti)

Move off a bit and don't stand in my sunlight, I tell you, cynic in a tub,
finish off any bird of mine foolish enough to venture out
between morning and night, since I have no other jester for you,
and another creature crows at me, another less false idol whispers:
all that shattered water, indecisive brother, dawn's daughter, is like
an entrapping mirror, one more gleam between coin and shroud,
but you're the gods' flea, it tells me, no bright light, no congenital beast,
and as for the thread of black sea in your bucket, I've seen it
quenched, I've touched the body's primitive proxy, listless lady,
the scuffling world has its reasons, how they flock, doling out
mystery for machination: a golden age, that'll never catch on,
warmly welcome the dog—Diogenes? or the disguise, grimace and
    wink, of a tuxedoed publicist?,
from time to time my featherless biped preaches populism, acid love
for each other, listen, how he calls it out from the podium,
his supreme *befores*, purity of a different regime, how he shears
with his serge, his empty sack, his parchments all in vain,
although I heard the coins clink, I think to make amends, applause,
going pulpit to pulpit, speechifying about flame itself, ritual and red,
charging time for what's left over, my fortune teller, ironwork or street,
a truth I do not know, over here, I repeat, in this provincial
maze, where my brother braids, district daughter, his opportunistic
smoke with one crazy gesture: there's a thought!, and devises conventional
endings, my lady, reading, his plausible coinage in the air
may transmute values, clear out ideas with an example, or at least
lucidly postpone them, in whose favor?,

mejor ya me miro,

agua,

irme.

better to watch myself,

water,

as I go.

CPSIA information can be obtained at www.ICGtesting.com
Printed in the USA
LVOW07s0807080416

482496LV00002BA/2/P